For Bishop Kenneth Goodson—
with highest regards
and Best Wishes

Sterling Staudemire
3/24/1977.

Christian Doctrine

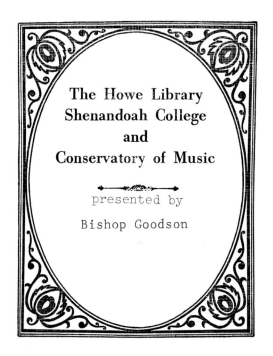

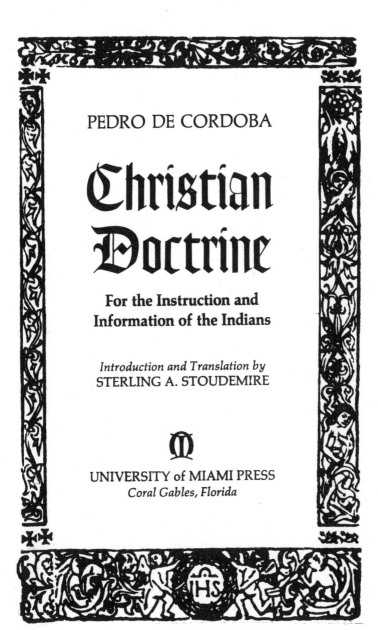

PEDRO DE CORDOBA

Christian Doctrine

For the Instruction and
Information of the Indians

Introduction and Translation by
STERLING A. STOUDEMIRE

UNIVERSITY of MIAMI PRESS
Coral Gables, Florida

Designed by Bernard Lipsky
Manufactured in the United States of America

Et diliges Dominum Deum tuum ex
toto corde tuo, et ex tota anima tua,
et ex tota cogitatione tua, et ex tota
virtute tua. Hoc primum mandatum.
Et secundum simile hoc: Diliges
proximum tuum ut teipsum. Majus horum
aliud mandatum non est.

Mark 12: 30-31

For
Mary Arthur Stoudemire

Contents

Preface

IN 1512, Ferdinand the Catholic, King of Aragon, Castile, Leon, Sicily, Naples, the Lowlands, Lord and Master of a large part of the New World, could not believe the scandalous reports brought officially to his attention regarding the rebellious acts of a young vicar of the Dominican order in Española, the Spanish Island, named by Columbus in 1492, and now Haiti and the Dominican Republic. This young upstart, with the aid of his zealous assistants, was at the point of destroying the social organization it had taken Spain twenty years to develop. And Ferdinand did not have Isabel to advise and console him for she had died in 1504.

The small community of the Order of Preachers, late in 1510, had begun to protest bitterly and firmly, but with dignity, the treatment of the Indians at the hands of the Spaniards. The king regularly received news and advice from clerics as well as his ministers. He was deeply shocked, however, by two sermons that had been preached a little more than a year before. The first sermon was a bill of particulars on Spanish atrocities and the second, which came a week later, had been advertised as something of a retraction designed to calm Spanish fury in Española. The retraction turned out, instead, to be a positive reaffirmation of the first sermon, a confirmation of Dominican position regarding the Indians. The two sermons placed full blame upon the governor, Diego Colón, son of Christopher Columbus and his successor as Admiral of the Ocean Sea. To King Ferdinand such rebellion and impertinence were unspeakable, even unthinkable.

The young Dominican vicar was Friar Pedro de Córdoba. The preacher was his chief assistant, Friar Antón Montesino, since that time referred to by historians as Antonio de Montesinos, a more common and modern name. The Dominicans had arrived in Española in 1510 to formally establish the Order of Preachers in the New World, but before very long they had made trouble for the governor, his treasurer, and almost every Spaniard on the island. Their only supporters were the Indians.

The first sermon was preached on the fourth Sunday in Advent, according to Las Casas[1] and may have been the first serious public pronouncement in America on civil rights. It was indeed a strong pronouncement on human rights. King Ferdinand, venting his righteous and royal indignation on March 20, 1512, dispatched a letter to Governor Diego Colón and acknowledged receipt of a report on the sermons. He made it clear that his theologians and scholars had informed him that there was no justification in canon law for Montesinos' heretical remarks. The king reminded his subjects, through the governor, that he and the late Queen Isabel had ordered the Indians to serve the Christians, in fact to be their slaves, and that this decision had been supported by his Holiness, Pope Alexander VI. The king further ordered the governor to inform the Dominicans that if they continued such a policy of disturbance, they would be returned to Spain for punishment.

The problem was not simple. Ferdinand did not realize that he was dealing with an unusual young friar. Seldom had he encountered a man possessed of such religious zeal and toughness of moral fiber. The Dominicans voluntarily returned to Spain to file a protest with King Ferdinand and, as a result, they were able to obtain certain modifications in the famous *Laws of Burgos* that had been promulgated in 1512. The 1513 revision and additions, however, offered the Indians only small protection from Spanish oppression.

But Pedro de Córdoba did not surrender to the established system, and few men of the church have accomplished so much as the friar did in only ten years in the New World. Yet, he remains relatively unknown except to serious students of early American history, to friars in the Order of Preachers, and to citizens of the Dominican Republic. Of all his accomplishments, the most far-reaching was in persuading Bartolomé de las Casas to give up his land and slaves and to become a Dominican. It is a great irony that Las Casas, selected to carry on the work of Córdoba, should come to be one of the most influential men of his day and, indeed, one of the best known and most controversial personalities in Spanish and American history, then and now. Pedro de Córdoba lies in an unmarked grave in the courtyard of the Dominican monastery in Santo Domingo.

The Las Casas bibliography assembled by the distinguished historians Lewis Hanke and Manuel Giménez Fernández, published in 1954, is an exciting and thorough work. Since that date many important studies on Las Casas have appeared, several by Professor Hanke alone. Las Casas came to the New World in 1502, perhaps already a priest. He returned to Spain, then went to Italy, and returned to Cuba where he was not long in acquiring both land and slaves. When Córdoba suggested that the Indians were not being treated properly, it was Las Casas who was one of the first to propose that Negro slaves might be imported into the colonies to assume some of the burden. But Las Casas' attitude toward slavery, especially with regard to the Indians, changed abruptly. He sold his land and slaves and joined the civil rights crusade, already well under way, led by Pedro de Córdoba. Sometime later (the exact date is not known) Las Casas took the habit of the Order of Preachers. He was the first to do so in America. He became so zealous regarding the welfare of the Indians that he made several trips to Spain imploring the king to establish better working conditions for them. His approach to this delicate matter was along the lines that Aristotle had set down, although not too clearly: some peoples are born, really created, to be slaves.

Negroes were in the category of slaves; Indians were not. The change of Las Casas from slave holder to protector of the Indians is complete and convincing. He could have lived from the sweat of his black slaves now that the Indian population of the islands had been sadly reduced in numbers. The young Dominican, however, pointed out that his life was most unchristian, unthinkable, and absolutely intolerable in a priest. This was the turning point in the career of Las Casas.

In addition to his role as champion of the Indians, Córdoba wrote the short catechism *Doctrina Cristiana,* usually referred to as the "short doctrine" or "catechism." Because it was simpler than other catechisms, particularly the longer, more sophisticated catechisms of Jean Gerson, famous French theologian of the fifteenth century, and Bishop Zumárraga, it was the one used to initiate the Indians into Catholicism. Córdoba's *Christian Doctrine* was used in various parts of the New World for at least twenty years before it was printed in Mexico in 1544 under the sponsorship of Bishop Zumárraga and at the printing establishment of Juan Cromberger that was managed by Juan Pablos. Pedro de Córdoba had died in 1521.

This little book should prove of more than passing interest to students of early American history, the Church in America, the Dominican order, and the beginnings of the civil rights struggle on this continent. It is one of the documents employed by the Dominicans in establishing their religions and their language in the West Indies, two jobs they did remarkably well. I would hope that the English version of the *Doctrina Cristiana* may be read by persons not acquainted with the Spanish language and Spanish-American history. I have, therefore, included in the introduction a short biography of Pedro de Córdoba as well as a brief account of the *Laws of Burgos* and related matters that may assist in placing the *Christian Doctrine* in proper perspective.

Many persons in widely separated places have given generously of their time and knowledge in assisting the writer in compiling notes for a biography of Pedro de Córdoba. Only the broad aspects appear here. It is hoped and planned that a complete biography will follow. I want to express my gratitude first to the Biblioteca Nacional in Madrid for its fine Spanish-American Collection, and to the staff of the Rare Book Room, especially to Don Francisco Pérez. I also recognize my large debt to Don Francisco Esteve Barba (Q.e.p.d.), chief of the Sección de Mapas in this library. The staff of the Instituto Fernández de Oviedo has been always ready to assist anyone interested in Hispanic-American subjects. Don Cirialo Pérez Bustamante, Don Ramón Ezquerra, and Doña Isabel de la Peña y Macía, director, secretary, and librarian respectively, have made it pleasurable to investigate the life of Pedro de Córdoba in their library. The running bibliography in the preface of Don Emilio Rodríguez Demorizi's facsimile edition of the *Doctrina Cristiana* has been of the greatest help; it is the most nearly complete Córdoba bibliography yet compiled. My special thanks go to Professor Lewis Hanke for his enlightening work on Bartolomé de las Casas and related subjects. The staff of the University of North Carolina Library and that of the John Carter

Brown Library of Brown University have been most generous with their help.

I am indeed grateful to several friends among the clergy who have helped find the proper theological phrase for my basic English translation.

I know that I have failed to find significant references to Pedro de Córdoba, and would welcome additional information on this fascinating man.

Sterling A. Stoudemire

Chapel Hill, North Carolina
June, 1970

Introduction

IN 1510 Spanish readers were elated over a new novel of chivalry, *The Heroic Deeds of Esplandián*, "legitimate son of Amadís of Gaul," whose fantastic deeds had been put in print for the first time two years before and had come to be a best seller. The *Deeds of Esplandián* did not receive the reprieve won by the father in the famous episode of the examination of the books in chapter six of the first part of *Don Quixote*, and was the first to go flying through the window to the courtyard to build the bonfire. The *Deeds of Esplandián*, in a way, received another sort of immortality. Since it was read as if it were a true account of exploration in some faraway Arcadia called California, it is not surprising that Spanish conquistadores should have chosen that name for the beautiful land they had just found on the coast of the South Sea in the New World. To early Spanish explorers, it was always the

South Sea, not the Pacific, and always the Ocean Sea, not the Atlantic.

In this same year (1510) Julius II was Pope, sponsor of both Raphael and Michael Angelo, and Martin Luther had been sent by his Augustinian order to Rome where he was scandalized by the spiritual laxity he found in high ecclesiastical places. The year before, Joanna the Mad, mother of Emperor Charles V, had been taken prisoner to Tordesillas where she was to remain almost half a century; Christopher Columbus had been dead four years, Queen Isabel, six; Charles, to become emperor, was ten years old, and the boy who was to become Francis I of France was sixteen years old. Henry VIII had been king of England one year; Erasmus was at the peak of his influence; Cardinal Jiménez de Cisneros was engrossed in his new University of Alcalá and in the *Complutensian Bible* his scholars were putting together.

And the year 1510 was an important date in the history of man's treatment of his brothers, for it was in that year that the Dominican order, under the direction of Fray Pedro de Córdoba, was established in Española, the Spanish Island, so named by Columbus on his first voyage and now the Dominican Republic and Haiti.

Pedro de Córdoba, Order of Preachers

FRAY Bartolomé de las Casas, then and now the most controversial figure connected with Spain in the New World, gives the longest contemporaneous account of the life of the Dominican Pedro de Córdoba, with whom he was closely associated for a number of years. There is no reason to doubt what the later Bishop of Chiapas has to say about the young Dominican who had been selected to establish the Order of Preachers in America. I will append other biographical data, assembled by later historians, to the general framework established by Las Casas.

In 1510, perhaps in the month of September, Providence brought the Order of Saint Dominic to Española. The prime mover in this significant event was Fray Domingo de Mendoza, brother of Fray García de Loaysa, who was to become general of the order, confessor to Charles V, archbishop of Sevilla, and president of the powerful Council of the Indies. Domingo de Mendoza was a well-educated cleric who knew the writings of Saint Thomas Aquinas almost by heart. When Mendoza decided to establish the Order of Preachers in the New World, he found a young man endowed by God with excellent spiritual and intellectual gifts. His choice was a native of Córdoba, of noble and Christian birth, tall and handsome, of excellent judgment, prudent, and at all times in complete control of himself. He was Fray Pedro de Córdoba.

Pedro de Córdoba had entered the Order of Saint Dominic at the famous Convent of San Estéban when he was still a student at the University of Salamanca. This convent was to train many distinguished clerics and to move into new quarters just about the time Córdoba came to the end of his career. The student Córdoba took advantage of every opportunity to study art, philosophy, and theology and had the reputation of being a learned and deeply religious friar. He imposed upon himself such rigorous penance that he suffered physical pain almost every day of his short life. Included in the original group sent to Española were Fray Antón Montesino (now known as Antonio de Montesinos), Fray Bernardo de Santo Domingo, and a lay brother. Pedro de Córdoba was named vicar of the group even though he was the youngest, only twenty-eight years old. The lay brother returned to Spain, but the others remained and became a powerful influence for Christianity, law, and order.

When the friars reached Española they were received by a devout Christian named Pedro de Lumbreras who gave them a hut in the corner of his corral, since no houses were available except those made of straw. Lumbreras supplied them with cassava bread, a few eggs from time to time, and an occasional piece of fish. The friars ate cabbage without oil, cooked with only Indian pepper, and, in general, lived in the greatest strictness. They had no bread made of wheat and were able to obtain wine for Mass only with great difficulty. Their beds were made of boughs and straw, and their rough cloth undergarments were covered by coarse wool tunics.

When the Dominicans reached Española, the second Admiral, Diego Colón, and his wife, Doña María de Toledo, had gone to visit friends in the city of Concepción de la Vega. Since Pedro de Córdoba was anxious to report his arrival, he and his companions traveled a distance of thirty leagues over rough and rocky terrain, eating cassava bread, drinking water from the streams, and sleeping on the ground with only their capes to cover them. Admiral Colón and his wife received them with respect and friendliness. The next Sunday was the octave of All Saints, and Pedro de Córdoba preached a sermon "on the Glory of Heaven that God has prepared for his chosen people." Las Casas reports that the sermon was delivered with great fervor and zeal, and that he considered himself fortunate to hear it. The vicar admonished his audience to go home after the sermon and, after they had eaten, to send to the church all the Indians that served them. The Indians came, men, women, and children; and Pedro de Córdoba, sitting on a rough bench and holding a crucifix in his hands, began to speak with the assistance of interpreters. In simple language, he gave the biblical account of the Creation and the story of the life of Christ, with special emphasis on the Crucifixion, Resurrection, and Ascension. Las Casas says that the sermon was inspiring, not only to the Indians but to the Spaniards who had returned to hear it.[2]

The Dominicans were not long in discovering the abject slavery of the Indians, the unspeakable hardships they endured and long hours they were forced to labor, a kind of living that soon resulted in many Indians dying. The Spanish masters' reaction to their slaves' mortality rate seems to have amounted merely to a concern over a diminished labor force. The Dominicans were strong in their statements that the Spaniards looked upon the Indians as lower animals, that the masters were unmercifully cruel and interested only in becoming rich. Within fifteen or sixteen years almost all the island Indians had died because they had been forced to work the mines and perform other exhausting tasks to which they were not accustomed.

Something quite unexpected made it possible for the Dominicans to be most effective in their work with the natives. A Spaniard named Juan Garcés had stabbed his wife to death because he believed she was involved in an adulterous love affair. The woman was a member of one of the prominent families of Concepción de la Vega. Juan Garcés fled into the jungle where he remained almost four years. One night he appeared at the crude monastery and begged the friars to accept him as a lay brother. He promised to devote his life to the service of God. Convinced of his sincerity and through their charity, the Dominicans accepted Juan Garcés as one of their number, and he proved to be of inestimable value to his brothers, because he had learned fluently several Indian languages during his years in the jungle. The friars were aware of the conditions under which the Indians worked, but they had not dreamed of the brutality that Garcés described. They considered the matter at great length, and finally the Dominicans came to the conclusion that they were compelled to condemn the atrocities from the pulpit. It was the least, they said, they could do as Christians. They selected the subject for the sermon, and in order to avoid the possibility that the audience would accept the sermon as the personal feeling of the preacher, the friars all signed their names to the document, showing their intent and unanimity. It was natural for them to select Fray Antonio de Montesinos to preach the sermon, for he was their most eloquent and persuasive speaker. Since it was the

Advent season, they decided to preach the sermon on the fourth Sunday, most certainly because of the Gospel appointed for that day. Almost everybody in the city of Santo Domingo came to Mass, including, as was expected and routine, the governor of the island, officers of the Crown, jurists, and other people of importance. Word had been passed throughout the area that a sermon would be preached in the main church and that it would be of interest to everybody, and it was further insinuated that it would be wise for everybody to come to hear it.

When the time came for the sermon, Fray Antonio de Montesinos went up into the pulpit and announced his text: "Ego vox clamantis in deserto" (John 1:23), now the gospel appointed for the third Sunday in Advent. After a few introductory remarks on the meaning of Advent, Montesinos plunged into a violent attack upon the Spaniards for the blindness in which they lived. He said that he had been sent to that island by Christ, that he was the voice of God crying in the wilderness. He insisted that the Spaniards were living in mortal sin, and that they would die in sin and go to hell as punishment for the cruelties and tyranny they had demonstrated toward the Indians. He pointed out that the Indians were required to work in the mines until they were unable to stand, that they did not receive proper food, that their illnesses went unnoticed, and that they were forced to work until they died. Montesinos insisted that the Spaniards were interested only in the amount of gold each Indian could dig out of the soil each day. The preacher went on to ask the Spaniards if they did not think the Indians were men and rational beings, and if the Spaniards were not obligated to love them as they loved each other. He asked them if they understood what he was saying, and if they were sorry for their behavior.

The Spanish audience sat stunned by these words. When the sermon was over, the preacher stepped proudly down from the pulpit. People could be heard muttering and mumbling to each other as they left the church. After they had gone home and finished dinner, almost every person in town made his way to the home of Governor Colón. They insisted that the governor punish the preacher for his sermon. Pedro de Córdoba explained that the preacher had expressed the opinion of all the Dominicans, not his alone, and he further made it clear that they intended to stand united in the views they held on this serious matter. The governor informed the Dominicans that if they did not apologize for their actions, they would be sent back to Spain. The vicar explained that it would be an easy task for the friars to return to Spain since they had very few possessions to carry with them. They had their missals and a few books; everything they owned could be placed in two small chests. After much discussion it was agreed mutually that Montesinos would preach the next Sunday. Word got around town that the preacher would repudiate what he had said the Sunday before, that he would offer an apology to the governor and the whole community for the unrest that had been the result of the previous sermon. Everybody seemed to be happy at the prospect.

Next Sunday came and the time for the sermon, and

the friar walked up into the pulpit and announced his text: "Repetam scientiam meam a principio, et sermones meos sine mendatio esse probabo" (Job 36:3). "I shall repeat from the beginning what I have already said, and I shall prove that my words are true." The congregation realized immediately that they had been trapped and that Montesinos was going to preach, in the main, the same sermon he had preached the Sunday before. Indeed, he repeated almost everything he had said the week before, only this time his observations were couched in even stronger terms. When he had finished the sermon, he came down from the pulpit and went to his monastery. The people sat stunned as they had been the week before. Once again they began muttering and grumbling and were even more inflamed against the troublesome Dominicans who would destroy their new society.

The governor decided to send a letter to King Ferdinand by the first ship that sailed and outline in detail what the Dominicans had done since they reached the island; how they had outraged almost every citizen; how they had condemned everybody to hell; how they threatened to completely upset the Spanish system. Naturally, the letter provoked a sensational reaction in Spain. The king summoned the provincial of the Order of Preachers in Castile and demanded an explanation, something the head of the order could not do. In the meantime, in Española, the governor decided to send Alonso del Espinal, a deeply religious, but not too bright, Franciscan, as messenger to the king to explain what had happened from the anti-Dominican point of view. When the Dominicans realized that a rival Franciscan was being sent to Spain to file an official report, in a sense betraying the Dominicans, Pedro de Córdoba thought it wise and necessary to represent both his own and the Dominicans' point of view to the king. Father Antonio de Montesinos was chosen for the mission, a logical choice since he had preached the sermon that sparked the bitter argument. The Dominicans did not have enough money to pay for the food Montesinos would eat on the return voyage, and it was necessary for members of the order to go around town begging the few maravedís necessary for this expense. Several charitable persons were willing to contribute to this worthy cause, but it was all too clear that they wished to remain unthanked and anonymous. Such a situation had not arisen before, and no one could guess what the consequences might be.

Upon his arrival in Spain, Montesinos reported to the head of his order. Fray Alonso del Espinal, the Franciscan emissary, had already reached the court where he was received, so says Las Casas, as if he were the Archangel Gabriel himself. Whenever Espinal came into the king's presence, a chair was brought in so that the friar could sit down. The king and the queen felt great friendship and affection for the Franciscans. Isabel was particularly devoted to them. As late as her last will and testament, she made it more than clear that if the Royal Chapel, then under construction in Granada, should not be completed by the time of her death, her remains were to be deposited in the Franciscan monastery in whatever city she was in when she died. The king repeated his earlier judgment that the Indians should work for the Spaniards, that they should continue to mine gold for their masters, and that he saw no good reason to change the practice that had been established and that he had decreed. When Montesinos reached the court, it was common knowledge that he had come to dispute the statement made by Espinal. Every time Montesinos got as far as the king's chamber, he was turned back, the door was closed, and he was told that the king was too busy to see him.[3] When the provincial of the Order of Preachers learned what was going on at court, he wrote to Vicar Pedro de Córdoba and explained the atmosphere that existed in Ferdinand's presence. Pedro de Córdoba decided to go to Spain to report to the king just exactly what was going on in Española and to give aid and comfort to his brother Antonio de Montesinos. When he reached Spain, he naturally reported to the provincial of his order and proceeded to court, which was at that time in Valladolid. He found that the *Laws of Burgos*, outlining Spanish policy toward the Indians, had just been promulgated (December 27, 1512). Córdoba saw in these laws small relief for the Indians, and there was even the possibility of complete annihiliation under the new code. He was courageous and frank enough to say that the laws were not acceptable in the form in which they had been written, and he spoke with the king at great length on the desirability, even the dire necessity, for modification and revision. The king asked Córdoba to take the laws under review and to make a recommendation for a possible adjustment. Ferdinand implied that there was a possibility of certain changes. Many people were consulted in the matter, and Córdoba made his recommendation, and on July 28, 1513, certain modifications were made. Las Casas was of the opinion that these slight improvements could not have been obtained if it had not been for the intercession and insistence of Pedro de Córdoba. Córdoba, however, felt that the changes were not sufficient, and he saw in the laws small protection for the helpless natives.[4]

Córdoba wanted to extend the work of the church to the mainland, and the king gave his permission for him to do so. Several Dominicans returned with Córdoba to Española to participate in the new mission, and several friars were sent ahead to the mainland to establish a crude monastery as working headquarters. At first the natives received them in a most friendly manner. But a Spanish ship arrived, manned by a crew lusting for gold, and an Indian cacique, his wife, and seventeen relatives were enticed aboard the ship and carried away. The Indians demanded the return of their chief and the people who were with him. When this request was not honored, the Indians attacked the innocent Dominicans, killing all who were there. When Córdoba learned of the slaughter of his advance guard, he felt that this tragedy should be no barrier to further efforts to establish a community on the mainland; rather, it was even greater incentive to carry the Christian religion to these ignorant people. He decided to lead the group personally and took with him Antonio de Montesinos, Juan Garcés, several other Dominicans, and a group of Franciscans who had just arrived from Normandy and who wished to establish a monastery of their order in the same area. Having no common vernacular, the Dominicans and Franciscans conversed in Latin. They established two communities several miles apart, and trouble was not long in coming. The Franciscans were massacred by hostile natives; of the Dominicans, only Córdoba and Montesinos survived and were able to return to Española under conditions that led later historians, as we shall see, to speak of miracles. The lay brother Juan Garcés, who had promised to devote his life to the work of the Dominicans, was one of those martyred.[5]

Las Casas says that in May 1521, on the vigil of Saint Catherine of Siena, Pedro de Córdoba died at the age of thirty-eight, in the Dominican monastery in Santo Domingo. Years of fasting and abstinence and, finally, tuberculosis brought on his death. His funeral was held the next day, on the feast of Saint Catherine of Siena, herself a beloved Dominican. It is not surprising that the preacher was Friar Antonio de Montesinos. He chose as his text "Quam bonum et quam iucundum habitare fratres in unum" (Psalms 133:1). These two brothers had lived together in peace and harmony, but they had found it difficult to teach Spaniards to believe that Indians were included among their brothers. At the end of the Mass, the body of Pedro de Córdoba was laid to rest in the courtyard of the small monastery.[6]

Spanish archives, especially the Archivo de Indias in Sevilla, are rich in documents on the early history of Española, long the center of Spanish operations in the New World. Many of these works describe the early

29

work of various religious orders, including the mission of Pedro de Córdoba and his struggle to establish his order firmly in a new land. In a letter dated Burgos, March 20, 1512, almost a year before the promulgation of the *Laws of Burgos*, King Ferdinand wrote the governor of Española, Diego Colón, concerning the sermons preached by Antonio de Montesinos. He insisted that there was no justification, theological or legal, for the heretical remarks made by the impassioned friar, and he directed the governor to advise the Dominican to refrain from making such statements, in or out of the pulpit, under penalty of return to Spain.[7]

A letter signed by Pedro de Córdoba and eight other members of his order, written before 1516 and perhaps as early as 1513, offered the Crown the opinion that it was contrary to human and natural law to hold the Indians in a system of forced labor that amounted to slavery. This letter also carried the startling suggestion to the Crown that Negro slaves should be sent to Española in order to reduce the work load and, consequently, the hardships imposed upon the Indians. Pedro de Córdoba was quite positive in his insistence that he had been sent by God to the New World. "... fui requisito ex parte Dei tamquam per eum adjurat in illo."[8]

In response to King Ferdinand, Miguel Pasamonte, treasurer of Española, on November 23, 1514, sent his Majesty a letter explaining exactly how the distribution of Indians had been made and listed each Spanish owner by name, telling how many *indios* or *indias* each had received. One of the revealing entries is: "Don Diego

Colón, the uncle of the admiral, has been assigned the chief Diego Leal de Aranda, along with 166 servants."[9]

In a letter written about the time of the death of Ferdinand (1516), Pedro de Córdoba makes a significant reference to Bartolomé de las Casas. He says that God had awakened the spirit of a young cleric who had gone to Spain to tell King Ferdinand of the deplorable situation in the New World and that after the death of the king, he had negotiated with the Crown's cardinal in seeking some solution to their problem. Not satisfied with the answers received, Las Casas had made still another trip to Spain hoping to obtain protective regulations for the Indians. Córdoba goes on to say, "He is a man of integrity and truth, a person who has lived in these lands many years and knows the area thoroughly."[10]

The Dominicans did not let the king forget that conditions in Española had not changed sufficiently to satisfy them, and Córdoba and other Dominicans were signatories to other letters, one of them dated June 4, 1516, repeating the shocking story of Spanish atrocities and begging for relief.[11]

Later Historians

THE most important sixteenth-century historian to recount the work of the Dominicans in Española is Gonzalo Fernández de Oviedo, who had been a passenger on the famous fleet of Pedrarias Dávila that sailed from Spain for Española, April 11, 1514, and who was to spend most of his next fifty years in the New World. The first part of his famous *History of the Indies* was published in 1535; the second part in 1557, about the time of his death. Oviedo was well acquainted with Las Casas and came to be his archenemy because of their conflicting views on Indian and Spanish colonial policy. (An oversimplification would stress that Las Casas had the romantic idea that all Indians were good; Oviedo took them for what they were, some good, some not so good.) He wrote at great length about Las Casas and the Dominicans but never mentioned Pedro de Córdoba. In many places in his voluminous writings, however, he describes what seems to be Córdoba's mission in the New World and especially his efforts to improve the lot of the Indians. He describes the convent in Santo Domingo where Córdoba lived and worked, and where Las Casas was to take the habit of Saint Dominic. He also mentions his split with Las Casas, whom he had earlier praised, and also describes the desperate efforts to establish Dominican and Franciscan communities on the mainland. In 1519, when news was received that Charles I of Spain had been elected emperor, Oviedo was in Barcelona—it was in this year that his novel of chivalry, *Claribalte*, was published in Valencia—and his description of the failure of the missions had to be taken from hearsay or secondary sources. He says that in an uprising of the Indians all but two of the Dominicans were massacred.[12]

San Juan de la Cruz, also a member of the Order of Preachers, describes how the convent of San Estéban in Salamanca sent several friars to America in 1510.

Antonio de Montesinos and Bernardo de Santo Domingo were in the group. He describes the sermon preached by Montesinos and gives much detail concerning the efforts to establish missions in Cuba and on the mainland at Cumaná, and he tells how Pedro de Lumbreras, the king's treasurer, assisted them in all these missionary ventures. He goes into detail regarding the ill-fated communities established by the Dominicans and their new Franciscan friends from Lombardy. He reports bluntly that all the friars except Pedró de Córdoba and one other were killed by the Indians.[13]

The writings of Fernández de Oviedo and Las Casas were available to, and used by, most sixteenth-century historians, even though the chief works of Las Casas were not published until much later. Agustín Dávila Padilla, born in Mexico and descended from Spanish conquistadores, compares Pedro de Córdoba with Friar Pedro Delgado, stating that even the wind and the waves seemed to obey him. He describes how Córdoba went to Margarita, an island just off the cape at Cumaná, Venezuela, with two ships. At first the Indians were friendly, and Córdoba ordered the masters to take the ships back to Española. Later, Dávila Padilla continues, there was an uprising, and the Indians killed all the friars except Córdoba and one other who was not identified. These two friars, each with a crude cross in his hands, made their way safely through the hostile band of Indians, and, reaching the coast, they found a ship with one mast (a vessel that had appeared miraculously) with Christ on the bow and Saint Dominic on the stern. This miracle produced such an effect upon the people that the Province of Santa Cruz placed on its coat of arms a ship with one mast with a crucifix on the prow, Saint Dominic on the stern, and two friars kneeling at the foot of the mast. Dávila Padilla gives the incorrect date of 1524 as the year of the death of Córdoba.[14]

Fray Antonio Remesal, like Pedro de Córdoba and San Juan de la Cruz, came from the convent dedicated to Saint Stephen, in Salamanca, where he took holy orders, March 13, 1593. (It should be remembered that in 1582 Pope Gregory eliminated ten days from the calendar and October 5 became October 15, in order to bring the vernal equinox back to March 21, as it had been decided at the Council of Nicaea in 325.) He came to America and is known throughout the New World as one of the leading historians of Dominican activities. His report on Pedro de Córdoba is essentially the same as that to be found in Las Casas. He says that when the news of Cortés' victory in Mexico reached Spain, there was a renewed burst of activity on the part of all religious orders to send missionaries to America. Quite often Remesal quotes Las Casas and Fernández de Oviedo without acknowledging the source.[15]

Another significant history of the early church in the New World is by the Franciscan, Gerónimo de Mendieta, who went to New Spain, the name given by the conquistadores to Mexico, in 1554, putting together his *Historia eclesiástica indiana* between 1573 and 1597. He bases his writings on both his own observations and the histories of Las Casas. This fine work was not published, however, until 1870.[16]

Antonio de Herrera, who also is a part of the scene,

was appointed official chronicler, May 15, 1596, and, by virtue of his position, all documents pertaining to the Indies had to be made available for his examination. Herrera also followed Fernández de Oviedo and Las Casas quite closely, but he put together perhaps the most readable synthetic history of Spain in America of that time. His story of Pedro de Córdoba is essentially that to be found in Las Casas.[17]

Luis Jerónimo Alcocer, who wrote in the seventeenth century, gives an interesting account of the Dominicans from their arrival in Española in 1510 to the death of Córdoba, and includes the abortive effort to establish missions in Venezuela and the miraculous return of Córdoba and one other friar on a ship manned by a crucifix on the foremast and Saint Dominic on the stern. His *Relación sumaria del estado presente de la Isla Española*[18] is in manuscript in the Biblioteca Nacional, Madrid. Several sections have been printed by Rodríguez Demorizi,[19] and in this same work,[20] as well as in the *Boletín del Archivo General de la Nación,* Rodríguez Demorizi has reprinted the section that recounts Córdoba's ability to trick the Indians into thinking that he and the devil had conversations in which the devil admitted that the Indians had been worshipping false gods and urged everyone to turn to the one and only God. Rodríguez Demorizi has taken this excerpt from González Dávila's *Teatro eclesiástico de la primitiva iglesia de las Indias Occidentales.*[22]

González de Acuña repeats the story of how Córdoba and others were sent to carry on their work in the lands already discovered and those that certainly would be discovered in the Indies. Even though his *Informe*[23] was in reality a report to the general of his order, he was alert to the fact that the document would be read by many people, and he did not hesitate to present the Order of Preachers in as glorious a light as it deserved. He quotes freely from Remesal, Dávila Padilla, Las Casas, Oviedo, and especially Luis de Páramo, whom he cites frequently.[24]

An interesting and rare work, and again one that leans upon Las Casas, Dávila Padilla, and quotes at length from Remesal, is *Isagoge histórica apologética de las Indias Occidentales,* published only in 1935 by Fernando Juárez Muñoz. This manuscript indicates that it was written in 1711, and goes on to relate the life of Pedro de Córdoba in Española, as told by other historians, stressing Córdoba's involvement with the *Laws of Burgos,* his attempts to establish a mission on the mainland, and his miraculous voyage from Cumaná to Española. He goes on to recount the story of Córdoba's death, repeating its date incorrectly as June 25, 1525.[25]

Beristain y Souza repeats the conventional information regarding Pedro de Córdoba, adding that Córdoba wrote many sermons but only the *Doctrina Cristiana* found its way to a printing press, and then only about twenty years after his death. Beristain knew only one copy of the catechism that was held in the library of the Franciscan fathers in Tezcucu; he also repeats the date of Córdoba's death as the vigil of Saint Peter.[26]

Ramón Martínez-Vigil reminds us that Dominicans had come to Española as early as 1495 with Columbus, but, he continues, Córdoba arrived in 1510 to establish a convent of his order. He repeats the story, now in the hands of almost every American historian, that Córdoba, Antonio de Montesinos, and Juan Garcés went to Venezuela in 1520 and were killed by the Indians.[27] Here he carries the story somewhat too far.

Francis Augustus MacNutt follows Las Casas' story regarding Córdoba but presents it in a more interesting and sprightly fashion. He, too, was unable to determine whether Las Casas entered the Dominican order before or after hearing Córdoba's sermon on the joys of Paradise.[28]

José Toribio Medina presents nothing new in the biography. He follows Las Casas, Remesal, and especially García Icazbalceta. He notes several death dates for Córdoba that have been mentioned by other historians and prefers to accept June 30, 1525. He states specifically, however, that Las Casas had said that the date was "las vísperas de Catalina de Siena, 1521."[29]

Serrano y Sanz expressed the opinion that the friars would not have been successful in their attempts to evangelize the American natives if it had not been for the support of the strong arm of the conquistadores. (The corollary must be that the conquistadores received equally as much support from the missionaries.) He repeats Pedro de Córdoba's ideal, that the society should be exclusively Indian, of course converted to Catholicism, with a minimum of aid from the king of Spain, and, most especially, supervised loosely and paternally by the friars who would be scattered over the entire area and sent into new places as they were discovered and settled.[30]

Henríquez Ureña says that it was Tomás de Berlanga,

provincial of the Order of Preachers in Española "who placed the Dominican habit on las Casas . . . about 1522." If this is true, it would indicate that Córdoba, who had been provincial, was already dead.[31]

Moreau de Saint-Méry tells us that in a church in La Vega, Santo Domingo, the first Mass was sung in the New World by Bartolomé de las Casas. He goes on to say that in 1517 the cardinal of Toledo, a Dominican and inquisitor general, commissioned as inquisitors the bishops of Santo Domingo and Concepción de la Vega. It was not until January 25, 1569, that the law opened the New World fully to the Inquisition.[32] We must bear in mind that the Inquisition was in the hands of the Dominican order, but the gentle friars in the New World strongly resisted attempts to establish the system in this hemisphere.

Quite understandably, contemporary historians of the Dominican Republic have been attracted to the wonderful stories, almost myths, regarding Pedro de Córdoba and his associates in Española, and these scholars, led by Emilio Rodríguez Demorizi and Pedro Henríquez Ureña, have published many articles in newspapers and journals that do not have wide circulation outside the island. A short history of the Dominicans can be found in Emiliano Tejera's article, "Gobernadores de la Isla de Santo Domingo, Siglos XVI-XVII,"[33] and in Emilio Rodríguez Demorizi's "Relaciones históricas de Santo Domingo."[34] Rodríguez Demorizi describes Córdoba as "one of the most distinguished figures in the church in America," and of Córdoba's age he says that he was "born in 1482 and died in 1521." He is quite positive regarding this date, as he should be, and in his facsimile edition of the *Doctrina Cristiana,* he repeats and stresses the statement made by Las Casas that Pedro de Córdoba died on the vigil of Saint Catherine of Siena.[35] It is unfortunate that García Icazbalceta in his *Bibliografía mexicana del siglo XVI* should place the date at 1525. His reputation as a scholar, as well as that of Millares Carlo, who reedited the bibliography, is of such high quality that it could well lead others to accept this more than questionable date.[36]

Marrero-Aristy, who methodically went about the task of trying to verify what Las Casas has written, has assembled much new information. Of perhaps forty thousand Indians who inhabited Española when Diego Colón assumed the governorship in 1509, only a few more than thirteen thousand remained in 1514. He says that in 1515 Córdoba and Montesinos found a formidable collaborator in Las Casas.[37]

It is understandable that Antonio de Montesinos should be studied more widely than Pedro de Córdoba; after all, his fiery sermon was the spark that set off a chain reaction that has not yet come to its end. Perhaps the best study of Montesinos is to be found in the excellent work of Lewis Hanke: *The Spanish Struggle for Justice in the Conquest of America.*[38] And the chain reaction, first activated in 1511, was to be seen and felt in various celebrations and testimonials on the four-hundredth anniversary (1966) of the death of Bartolomé de las Casas, thus fanning the smoldering embers of the "Black Legend"—the very unfavorable reputation Spain had gained as a result of Las Casas' report to Charles V in 1542 regarding Spanish atrocities in America. This *Very brief Account of the Destruction of the Indies* was translated into all principal European languages and was accompanied by the most horrible pictures of Spanish brutality, and used as anti-Spanish propaganda, although such attitudes existed in almost every European country. A celebration in Mexico was highlighted by three papers, October 24 to 26, 1966. The first was presented in the Academia Mexicana: "La idea antropológica del Padre las Casas," by Edmundo O'Gorman; the second and third in the Facultad de Filosofía y Letras: "Bartolomé de las Casas y la historiografía soviética," by Juan Antonio Ortega y Medina, and "El sacrificio humano en la *Apologética historia,*" by Teresa Silva Tena.[39]

Perhaps it is time for scholars to focus their attention upon Pedro de Córdoba and his followers and the good results they have achieved.

The Laws of Burgos

THE first "laws" outlining procedures to be followed by Spanish officials in the New World appeared in the form of letters and *cédulas* (orders) from the Crown to the responsible official. Only a few weeks before her death in 1504, Queen Isabel instructed her governor of the Indies, Nicolás de Ovando, to institute the encomienda system in Española.[40] Since the results desired by the queen were not achieved, the order was reissued by King Ferdinand, May 3, 1509, the year before Pedro de Córdoba established the Dominican order in Española. The Dominicans objected so violently to this system of land and slave holding that the Crown was forced to promulgate laws as guides for Spanish masters and owners. The first laws were made public in Burgos, December 27, 1512. The code was so meaningless and ambiguous that new objections were the chief result. Several additions and slight revisions were devised on July 28, 1513. These "laws" were based on Aristotle's hazy concept of natural slavery, a concept upon which all Spanish legislation for subject peoples was based.[41] These *Laws of Burgos* required Spanish officials to look to the spiritual welfare of the Indians. They should be taught the Ave Maria, Pater Noster, Creed, Salve Regina, and other prayers; they should learn to name the seven deadly sins, the Articles of Faith, and to know other basic Christian ritual. The Indians should be permitted to continue their traditional song-dance that they called *areito* throughout the islands, and they should always be well fed, have individual hammocks, and, after a certain time, wear clothes. The only actual protection in the first thirty-two laws (1512) was the general enjoinder that Indians were not to be used as beasts of burden, nor were they to be beaten. Pedro de Córdoba regarded the first laws as almost no protection for the Indians, and, at his insistence, five additional laws were promulgated in 1513, but only four were enacted: (1) an Indian woman could not be forced to work on the same job with her

41

husband; (2) children under fourteen years would not be permitted to do the work assigned to an adult, rather they should be employed in weeding the fields; (3) unmarried Indian girls would work with their parents, or where their parents permitted them to work; (4) within four years of the publication of the laws, all Indians would be required to wear clothes and be educated so that in time they would become sufficiently "civilized" to govern themselves. The Dominican ideal was self-government, with only benevolent supervision from Spain.[42]

The slight and only nominal protection afforded by these laws is the very motivation that kept the Dominicans, led first by Pedro de Córdoba and later by Bartolomé de las Casas, active in their fight for civil rights in America.

Pedro de Córdoba's "Christian Doctrine"

PEDRO de Córdoba's *Christian Doctrine* was published in Mexico in 1544 by the house of Juan Cromberger, with the permission and blessing of Bishop Juan de Zumárraga. For a long time this small catechism was regarded by some students of American history as the first book published in the New World.[43] It was not the first, but historians of printing are not sure of the title that deserves that distinction, and there is sharp disagreement on the matter. What is clear is that the more new information brought to light, the more clouded the origins of American printing appear. The picture is almost as confused as the story of the origins of printing in Europe. We do know that on June 12, 1539, Juan Cromberger contracted with Juan Pablos (Giovanni Paoli), a native of Brescia, Lombardy, to print books in Mexico City, the books to carry the imprint: "Printed in the great and most loyal city of Mexico, in the establishment of Juan Cromberger." The press was actually set up in the home of Bishop Zumárraga, and the first book, completed in 1539, could have been the first in America. Juan Cromberger died in 1542, and Juan Pablos continued to print books up to the time of his death in 1560.[44]

It is logical to assume that Pedro de Córdoba began to put together his *Doctrina Cristiana* shortly after his arrival in Española, for there was an obvious need for such a work, one of the important tools of the missionary. His first sermon, as Las Casas reports, was really an outline of the catechism that was not to be printed for thirty-four years, more than twenty years after the death of the author. The colophon states that it is a "beginning catechism," a sort of outline to be used with Indians who had received little or no instruction in Catholic dogma and Roman ritual.[45] Bishop Zumárraga gave full credit to Córdoba, but he does state that a few other things had been added by his associates in Mexico. It would be impossible to say what these additions are. It may be that they are limited to the several Aztec words which would make the whole work more intelligible to Mexicans. These words involve the names of Mexican temples and their gods.

Many books of Christian doctrine were published in Mexico in the first half of the sixteenth century, but only those having some relation to the work of Pedro de Córdoba have been considered here. Only five copies of his *Doctrina* are known to this writer: one each in the John Carter Brown Library of Brown University, the British Museum, the New York Public Library, the Library of the American Antiquarian Society, and the Library of the University of Texas. At one time the John Carter Brown Library held three copies. Mr. Brown secured the first copy at the Mondidier sale in 1851; later he was able to purchase a second copy; a third copy was acquired after his death from Nicolás León in 1896, the only remaining copy in this fine library. The Mondidier copy was exchanged with the American Antiquarian Society in 1946; the other copy was exchanged with the Lenox Library in 1898.

There can be no doubt that Córdoba's *Christian Doctrine* was intended for the instruction of beginners. Rarely has so much of the Bible and Catholic doctrine been reduced to such short space. In only sixty pages Córdoba includes the seven Articles of Faith, the Ten Commandments, the Seven Sacraments, Deeds of Mercy, how to make the sign of the cross, a sermon for those who have just been baptized, a brief history of the world from the Creation to the Ascension, and two blessings for the table (one before the meal and another after). Interestingly, both blessings are in Latin, the only Latin in the text.

All along the way the translator has felt that the clichés regarding translations are entirely inadequate to cover this case. The Italian "Traduttore ... tradditore," or "Faithful ... not beautiful; beautiful ... not faithful" in no way can apply to this case. This text is unusual for the early sixteenth century, and surprising, at first glance, as the work of a cleric who had received the best formal education and who had been steeped in a Latin environment since he was a boy. The text does not resemble the Spanish-Latin style that might be expected to come from the pen of a man in Pedro de Córdoba's position; nor does it resemble the rambling of the novels of chivalry that were the most popular secular reading of this age. The text is a confusion of sentences, lax punctuation, even for the Renaissance, and repetition, often in clause after clause, sentence after sentence. This small book was obviously meant to be given to the Indians verbatim. The author, understanding his audience, approached the subject as if he were addressing children. And indeed he was. One is reminded of Cervantes' demonstration of this well-known technique through the words of Sancho Panza in his delightful and mesmeric folktale about the goatherd (I,20): "There was a goat shepherd, I mean one who tended goats, and that shepherd or goatherd, as I say in my story, was named Lope Ruiz, and this Lope Ruiz was in love with a shepherdess named Torralba, and this shepherdess named Torralba was the daughter of a rich cattle breeder, and this rich cattle breeder. . . ."

Pedro de Córdoba, in spite of his Christian fervor and Catholic orthodoxy, understood that the Judeo-Christian story of the Creation, Flood, Ten Commandments, description of Heaven and Hell, the Nativity,

Crucifixion, and Ascension of Christ were so foreign to the Indian way of thinking, so contrary to his beliefs and superstitions, so different from the myths concerning his gods, that Spanish missionaries would be hard put to do the job they were sent to do. These narratives had to be put into simple language for simple people. It would be very easy to turn the Spanish of the *Doctrina Cristiana* into a literal English equivalent, and perhaps most of the original spirit would be retained, but to the modern reader the effect would be unpleasant, dangling, endless, and wholly unsatisfactory. Then arises the question as to how far a translator may go in converting the book into English, in "improving" the original. The consensus, lay and cleric alike, seems to indicate that the translation should hold as close to the original text as possible, in keeping with some standards of English syntax, in order to retain the flavor and spirit of the *Doctrina,* even though it is obvious that sixteenth-century conditions and the society of Española no longer can be reconstructed. I have, therefore, made very few editorial changes in the text. In long run-on sentences and series of clauses connected only by conjunctions, I have felt it proper to separate sections into separate sentences. After all, "and" and "or" were often the only punctuation marks in the early years of printing.

The translator hopes the reader will enjoy this little book that first brought Christianity and the Spanish language to large numbers of native Americans. I admire more each day the young Dominican who came to the New World in 1510. He had the courage to defy the strongest monarch of his age, and in the process he established the civil rights movement in America. He died at the age of thirty-eight and was buried in the courtyard of the Dominican monastery, in the spring of 1521. It was the day of Saint Catherine of Siena, the most famous female Dominican saint, who, along with Saint Teresa of Avila, according to reports circulating in the Vatican, will be made a "Doctor" in the Rόman Catholic Church, the first women to be admitted to the exclusive group of thirty men.

Indeed Pedro de Córdoba and Saint Catherine have a great deal in common: they devoted their lives to their fellows; they always worked for peace; they did not hesitate to question the top civil authorities. They both died when their mission was just beginning.

Christian Doctrine

by
Pedro de Córdoba

Mexico
Juan Cromberger
1544

Dotrina xp̃iana pa

inſtrucion ⁊ informació delos indios: por manera de hyſtoria. Compueſta por el muy reuerendo padre fray Pedro de Cordoua: de buena memoria: primero fundador dla orden delos Predicadores élas yſlas del mar Occeano: y por otros religioſos doctos dla miſma ordé. La ql dotrina fue viſta y examinada y aprouada por el muy. R. S. el licéciado Tello de Sādoual Inquiſidor y Uiſitador en eſta nueua Eſpaña por ſu Mageſtad. La qual fue empreſſa en Merico por mandado del muy. R. S. dó fray Juã çumarraga pmer obiſpo deſta ciudad: del cóſejo de ſu Mageſtad. ⁊c. y a ſu coſta. Año de. M.d.rliiij.

Có preuilegio de ſu. S. L. L. M.

Christian Doctrine

For the Instruction and Information of the Indians
In the Manner of History.
Composed by the Very Reverend Father
Friar Pedro de Córdoba
of Good Memory
First Founder of the Order of Preachers
in the Islands of the Ocean Sea,
and by Other Learned Monks of the Same Order.
This Book has been Seen, Examined and Approved by
The Very Reverend Licentiate
Tello de Sandoval[1]
Inquisitor and Inspector in this New Spain
on the Part of His Majesty.
It has been printed in Mexico by order of the Very Reverend Friar
Juan de Zumárraga[2]
the first Bishop of this City of the Council of His Majesty etc.
and at his cost.
The year of
MDXLIIII
I.H.S.
With permission of his Sacred, Catholic, Imperial Majesty.

My dearly beloved brothers:

I WANT you to know and to understand that we love you dearly and, through this love that we have for you, we have suffered great hardships in coming from distant lands and crossing wide seas. And we have subjected ourselves to many risks of death, in order to come to see you and to tell you about the great and marvelous secrets that God has revealed to us. We have come so that we may tell this to you, and so that we may inform you of the wonders that God has given us and of the great joys and pleasures that will be given us in Heaven. These joys and delights are of such quality that as soon as you learn about them and understand them, you will prize them more than all gold and silver and precious stones, and even more than all the wealth there is in the world. We beg you, therefore, to remain very attentive to our words and to try diligently to understand them, because they are the words of God. He has commanded us to tell you all this because He wants to make you His children so that He can give you the very great wealth, pleasures, and delights that you have never seen nor heard until now.

In order that you may come to know these great benefits and to enjoy such great delights and pleasures, you must know a very great secret that you have not learned or heard until now. It is that God created two places. One is above in Heaven, where you can find all the pleasures, wealth, and riches that one might imagine. There is no suffering there, no illness, pain, sadness, poverty, hunger, thirst, weariness, cold, heat, nor anything else which can cause us pain or sorrow. This place is called Glory or Paradise. The souls of all good Christians go to this place, which is so pleasant and filled with many riches. You and your souls will go there, too, if you will be friends of God, if you become Christians, and if you follow God and keep His commandments. The other place God located below in the very center of the earth. This place is called Hell. Souls of all people who do not believe in God and who are not Christians, and also the souls of bad Christians who do not keep God's commandments, will go there. In this place all evil things have been brought together, and a great fire is there that burns the souls of those who are not Christians and the souls of bad Christians. This fire never goes out nor is it ever extinguished. There souls forever suffer intense pain, illness, torture, great thirst and hunger, and great cold and heat. There the souls are burned in caldrons and pots filled with pitch, brimstone, and boiling rosin. There they are burned and roasted. And they experience other infinite sufferings that you could not even imagine. And this fire and this punishment never come to an end, for they last forever.

The souls of those who are not Christians, and of the bad Christians, once they enter this place, never are able to get out again. For this reason they are always weeping and moaning aloud and uttering loud cries because of the great pain and tortures that they experience. They burn continually in great flames of fire that never go out. And for this reason the suffering of the souls that enter there never comes to an end.

In that place, so bad and full of so many tortures, are all your people who have died and all your ancestors, parents, grandparents, relatives, and all who have existed and have passed from this life. You will go there, too, unless you become friends of God, and unless you are baptized and become Christians, because all who are not Christians are enemies of God. For this reason you should give thanks to God and serve Him willingly since He has done you such great kindness as to send us to you so that we might admonish you and teach you how you can be free from those torments of Hell, where all of your ancestors are now burning. And He has sent us so that we might put you on the road to the glory of Heaven to enjoy the great happiness and pleasure we have described. And He has also sent us in order to give you some idea of the blindness and error in which you have lived up to now, since you have not known your

Creator, the true God, nor have you served Him. You have gone about as men without intelligence or understanding who do not know what they do. Understand well that God has sent us to tell you who the real God is and also to teach you why God created you just as He created us.

You must know, therefore, that God created you, and also us, and everybody in this world, so that we might know Him, and knowing Him, love Him, and loving Him, He also will take us as His friends. And when we die, He will carry our souls to Heaven where there is glory and pleasure and happiness that He has prepared for the souls of His friends who are the good Christians, and also for you, if you should become Christians and desire to be friends of our great God. These blessings and pleasures never come to an end, and the souls that go to Heaven, to enjoy such happiness, never die nor do they grow old. They are always young and beautiful and merry and happy. And they dwell with God in great palaces that are very beautiful, decorated with roses and flowers, and painted in many different colors. And these palaces are filled with a pleasing fragrance.

There, in the house of our great God (and this house is the whole sky), there is an infinite number of servants who serve Him. Each of these servants has a beautiful palace for himself where he resides with his friends. Also in that house all good Christians will reside, and you will be there too, and each one of you will have another very beautiful palace, if you desire to be friends of this great God. And you will receive this friendship from Him if you believe in Him, and if you are baptized and become Christians, and if you learn all that Christians must know and believe, and if you obey them. We shall tell you what you must know and believe, and the commandments you must keep, so listen with all attention.

The Articles of Faith

FIRST, please know that for God to love you dearly, and for Him to carry your souls and bodies to Heaven, and for Him to lift you up to the place of His palace and large house, so that you may enjoy the great blessings and pleasures, it is first necessary for you to know God, and to know who God is, and what He is like. You must learn and believe fourteen things that we call the fourteen Articles of Faith. Anyone who wants to be a good Christian must learn and believe these Articles of Faith firmly, without any doubt whatsoever.

In the first Article of Faith you learn the nature of God.

The first Article, or the first acknowledgment, is to learn and to believe that there is only one all-powerful God, and that there are not many gods, nor more than one single God. And this God is all-powerful. He can do anything that He wants to do, and no one can do anything unless God gives him the power to do it. Nothing is done in Heaven or on earth without the command and will of this one and only God. And everything that He commands and wills, all this is done.

Here you must know that because of His command, the skies move, the sun rises, and the moon rises, and because of His command, they shed light upon the world. It is through His command that it rains, and through His command that the earth brings forth fruit, herbs, and flowers. Through His command people are born and die and live. Through His command springs send forth water, and rivers run with water. And it is through His command that Christians have come to this land. Because if this great God, who is the one and only God, did not will it, no Christian could come here. And through His command and will we come also to preach to you and to teach you. Because, as we have already said, this God, of whom we preach, is single and all-powerful, and He does anything that He wishes to do. And no one can do anything against His will.

This God has even a greater quality. He is immortal, for He cannot die. Nor can He suffer harm, illness, grief, fatigue, hunger, thirst, sorrow, or any other thing that would cause Him suffering. He is spiritual. He does not have a body, but He is very beautiful—so beautiful that there is no beauty in all the world that can be compared with the beauty of God. He is more beautiful than the sun and the moon and the stars, and even more beautiful than all the flowers and roses of the world and even, I say to you, more beautiful than all the beautiful things in Heaven and in earth joined together in one beautiful thing in which would be all the beautiful things of the world. This very beautiful thing would be ugly compared with the beauty of God.

You must know, therefore, that from this great

beauty of God proceed all other beautiful things, for He gives beauty and light to the sun and the moon, to the stars and roses and flowers and herbs and trees. In short, since He is so beautiful and resplendent, He gives splendor and beauty to all things.

In God are to be found all things that are perfect and virtuous.

In this great God are to be found all perfection, goodness, and power. He gives power to fire to shed light and to warm, to air to chill, to water to wet and cleanse and to breed fishes. He gives the earth power to produce herbs and trees and maize and fruits and all other things. He gives power to herbs to cure illnesses, and He gives taste to all things that are delicious.

Our great God is also very wise because He knows everything. He knows all that has taken place previously in the world, and He knows all things of the present that take place throughout the world, in Heaven as well as on earth. He knows the thoughts of all men; everything they think in their hearts, and He knows everything that is done in secret and in public, and everything that is done in Hell. And He knows everything that is to happen in the future.

Our God is also good because He sustains everything, small and great, that lives in the world, in the sea as well as on the earth.

Our God has been kind to man since He gave him the earth and the waters, and the birds, and everything in this world. And He gave him the sun to light him by day, and the moon and the stars by night. And He also gave him many other things. In exchange for all these things, God does not ask you to sacrifice your children, or kill your slaves, or any other living person, or cut your own flesh, or spill your own blood. He only wants you to love Him and honor Him as the true God, and not to consider any other as God, for there is no other God except Him. And those things that you worship as gods have no power. They cannot give you anything, because there is only one God. He is the one we preach to you, and He is very good. The gods you worship and honor as gods are only devils and evil enemies of the true God. The God whom we preach to you threw your gods from His house, as later we shall tell you, because they were evil, and they wished you ill. They ordered you to kill your children and your slaves and other persons, and they further ordered you to spill your own blood. But the real God of whom we preach, since He is good, loves Christians well, and will love you if you wish to be His friends. He does not want you to kill your children or your slaves, or any other person, nor does He want you to shed your blood unnecessarily.

Our God is also very large, because He is in Heaven and on earth and in the air, and here and in Castile and in all the world, although you do not see Him, because God does not have a body. Since He does not have a body, we cannot see Him with the eyes we have of the body; but the soul, which has no body, very easily can see Him after it leaves the body. Even though we do not see Him here, He is among us and gives us life. If He did not sustain our lives, we would die at once. He is in all things and supports them in their being, and gives them power to increase and multiply. In Heaven He displays

Himself to His friends, very clear and beautiful, where you and we shall see Him if you become His friends, and if you become Christians.

You should love this God who is so great and so powerful, so beautiful, so rich, and so good, and who loves mankind so much. And you should serve Him and take Him to be your God because there is no other God but Him.

And so you will recognize the deception in which you have lived by believing that Huizilopochtli[3] or Tezcatlipoca,[4] and others whom you regarded as gods, were gods. They were not gods, but evil demons who deceived you, as we shall explain later, since there is not in all the world or in Heaven or on earth or in the sea any God except the one and only God who rules and governs and sustains everything.

And this is the first Article that you must believe, so that you may go to Heaven to share and enjoy the pleasures that God has provided there for His friends.

And in order to understand three other Articles of Faith, of the thirteen that follow, you must know that just as man is of one nature, this nature is to be found in many persons, in me, and in each one of you and in all men. And thus many persons are of the same nature, as the nature of stone is in many stones, and they all have a nature which is called stone, so this might be said of all other things.

And thus God is of one nature, as has already been said, and is in many persons, to wit, in three:

The first person is called God the Father.

The second is God the Son, because He was engendered by the Father, not as other men are engendered, for He has no physical body, but as the sun engenders the rays that it produces.

The third person is called God the Holy Spirit, which proceeds from the Father and from the Son, as light proceeds from lightening and from the sun.

These three persons have one nature which is called God or Divinity. Many men, in the same way, have one nature which is called humanity, and many stones have a nature which is called stone. There is a great difference, however, between the nature of God and the nature of man, because men have a nature that is shared by all men, and the part that is in me is not in that person nor in this other one, and the part in that other one is not in me. And the same is true of other creatures. In God this is not the case, because the nature of God is not divided into three persons, in the Father, the Son, and the Holy Spirit, but is one single nature in the Father and in the Son and in the Holy Spirit. The Father and the Son and the Holy Spirit, therefore, have the same nature, because the nature that is in the Father is in the Son and in the Holy Spirit, without its being separated and divided. It is much as a garment of clothing or a piece of cloth is of one nature, and this cloth has many folds, and these folds all have one nature which is in the cloth. And the cloth has many folds and is not many different pieces of cloth, but one. So in God there are many persons, to wit, three, Father, Son, and Holy Spirit. There are not many gods, but one single true God. As the cloth that has many folds is not many cloths but one, even though it has many folds, and one fold is not another. God is one only and has many persons. And the one person is not the other nor is the other the first one, but each person really is different. And of these three persons one is called Father, another Son, and the other Holy Spirit. And all three compose one single God, as one single piece of cloth with a number of folds. And so in God there is one nature and three persons, and the three persons are not three Gods or three natures, but one nature and one God. And so it is with the waves of the river or of the sea, one wave is not the other nor is the other another, and so all three persons are one nature as the waves are all one nature. The person of the Father is not the person of the Son, nor is the person of the Father and the Son the person of the Holy Spirit. So this second acknowledgment or Article of Faith is to believe that He is the Father.

The third Article is to believe that He is the Son, as has been said.

The fourth Article is to believe that He is the Holy Spirit. And so these three persons, the Father which is God and Son which is God and the Holy Spirit which is God, are only one God and not three Gods. The Father is one God in three persons, and not one single person but one single substance.

The fifth Article of Faith is to believe that God is the creator of all things, and that He created everything from nothing. All of God's creatures are divided into three classes or differences. Some of them are only corporal, others spiritual, and still others are both corporal and spiritual. The corporal creatures, or the things that have body, are all those things that are recognized with the five senses, either with the eyes looking at them, or with the ears hearing them, or with the nostrils smelling them, or with the taste tasting them, or with the sense of touch touching them. These are called the five bodily senses.

The five senses recognize the heavens, the sun, moon, stars, fire, air, water, fishes, land, stones, all animals, and trees. All these things are called corporal because they have body, and also because they are recognized or perceived by the bodily senses. And not one of these things that I mentioned has any understanding. And all things in the world are corruptible and mortal, except the heaven, the sun, the moon, and the stars, which are not corruptible. They do not, however, have understanding or feeling.

The second creatures are spiritual for they do not have body. They are immortal and cannot die. They have better intelligence than ours. These creatures were created by the all-powerful God in Heaven. These creatures are called angels. God created all these angels in great goodness and honor and perfection and beauty. And God gave these angels His commandments so that they should obey them. Then there was division among the angels but most of them received the commandments of God and obeyed them. And God confirmed these angels in His grace and established them as His friends in His house and kingdom forever, and He gave each one a seat where he could sit and a very great palace in which he could reside.

The other group of angels, among whom there was

one who was more powerful than all the others, did not wish to accept the commandments which God gave them, nor did they want to obey. They were disobedient to God and did not wish to keep His commandments, so God took away from them His grace and His love and turned them into very ugly demons. Then God ordered the good angels to throw them out of Heaven, and the good angels fought with them until they threw them out of Heaven, and they fell below, and they did not stop until they had fallen to the very bottom of Hell. There they will remain, forever, in the fire and other tortures that are there, as we have told you before. This is the place where all those who are not Christians are going, and where the bad Christians also are going. Others of those evil angels, whom we now call devils or demons, remain here in this world among us.

The third creatures that God created are both corporal and spiritual, composed of both body and soul. These are men and women. And regarding this you must know two things: One is to learn why God created man, and the other is to know how He created and formed him.

In connection with the first matter which is to know why God created men and women, you must know that before all those evil angels who fell from Heaven were evil, each one had in Heaven his own chair in which he sat and each one had a very rich and beautiful house in which he lived. When they were thrown out of Heaven, all those chairs and houses remained vacant, and a large part of Heaven was unpopulated. God decided to create other creatures, therefore, in order to take them to

Heaven to fill those chairs and houses that were vacant. And so God created a man and a woman so that they might engender many others. And as they went on multiplying, God would take them, a few at a time, to Heaven until all those vacant places should be filled.

And you must know that before God created this man and this woman, He created all these things that we see in the world. And He created in the best part of the world a very pleasant place that He filled with all the good things there are in this world—all the fruits, roses, flowers, trees, and beautiful, savory, fragrant, and attractive things—the best that there are in all the world. He also created there a very large spring from which issues forth very powerful rivers, with which that place was watered; and it was very large. These rivers flowed from this place to water a large part of the earth. This spot is very delightful and surrounded by very high walls. It is called the earthly Paradise, which means flower garden or garden of pleasures.

After God created this beautiful flower garden and all the things that there are in this world, He decided to create a man and a woman.

The manner in which God created the man and the woman was as follows: First He created man. In order to do it, He took a mass of clay and formed from it an image of a very perfect man. And after He had formed it, He created a soul and placed it in that body that He made of clay. Then the man rose up a living and perfect man. And he was the most handsome and wise of all those that were, or ever would be, in the world. And God named this man Adam. And He took him from the place where He had created or formed him and placed him in that earthly Paradise, so pleasant and so beautiful. And as soon as he was there, God brought before him all the birds and animals that God had created so that that man, whose name was Adam, should give to each one of these animals the name that was most suitable. And Adam was so wise that as soon as he saw them, he recognized the nature and character of each one of them, and to each one he gave a name that suited it best, according to its nature. [30]

As soon as Adam had named the creatures, he looked very carefully and considered all the animals, for he wanted to find someone who would be similar to himself so that he would have a companion. But he did not find her. And when God saw that the man was alone He said, "It is not right for man to be alone. Let us make another creature that may be similar to him and who will be his helpmeet and his companion." Then He threw a great sleep upon Adam and made him go to sleep, and while Adam was asleep, God painlessly removed one of his ribs and formed from that rib a very beautiful and perfect woman. And when Adam awakened and saw her, he knew that she had been formed from his body, and he said, "This is flesh of my flesh and bone of my bones, for her man will forsake his father and his mother and live with his wife. She shall be called 'woman,' which means 'a thing made from man.'" And afterwards Adam named her Eve, which means "mother of all people." And God gave this woman to Adam as his lawful wife, and he married her, and they loved each other greatly as husband and wife.

And after this, God said to them, "Behold, my children, all the things that I have created in this world, animals as well as birds, plants, herbs, rivers, and fountains, and all the other things that you see. All these things I have created for your use, and I want you to make use of all of them, to be masters of them, and so shall all those who descend from you be their masters. Therefore, increase and multiply and fill the earth with people."

From these two persons, Adam and Eve, of whom you have heard, have descended all the people of the world. You and we are descended from one father and one mother who were Adam and Eve.

These two creatures, which are man and were created by God, are composed of both body and soul. So are all men and women of the whole world, for they all have descended from these two whom God first created. And you should know that when a father and a mother beget a child, they beget only the body, for only God creates the soul and places it in the body so the body will live. And so He does to everyone who is born in this world. The soul is immortal, for it can never die, just as the angels who are in Heaven also are immortal. And these souls are spiritual and have no physical form, but they do have understanding and power with which they can understand, see, hear, and know all things. All other souls of animals, birds, and fishes, and any others are mortal. They, in themselves, have no understanding, sight, hearing, or taste that is separate from the body. And when some animal dies, or when the animal is killed, it dies completely, both soul and body, but when a man or a woman dies, he or she does not die entirely, for only the body dies, and the soul remains alive forever, separated from the body. And when it is separated from the body, it understands, hears, sees, and can speak even more excellently than when it was in the body. And separated from the body it can receive joy, pleasure, and glory if it were good when it was in the body, and if it is found good upon its departure from the body. And it can also receive torture, suffering, and pain if it were evil while it was in the body. If it is found to be evil upon leaving the body, it will suffer along with the revived body. For when man is alive everything that he does, the soul does, and not the body alone. And for this reason after a man is dead, his soul remains alive and immortal, and will reap the reward and glory for the good deeds that it did when it was in his body. And, also, when the body is resurrected it will receive tortures and sufferings for its sins. Since they were companions in good and in evil, so they shall be sharers of glory or of suffering.

After God placed our first parents, Adam and Eve, in that earthly Paradise, and after everything happened that you have heard about, God said to Adam and to Eve, "You well know and see that I am your Creator and Lord who has created you. And I have put you in this delightful place, and I have made you master of all things that I have created in this world. It is right also for you to recognize me as your Lord and to be subject to me and to obey me. And you should accept and keep the law that I give you, so that by keeping this law, and obeying what I command of you, you may be preserved in this happy estate that you now have and merit even greater happiness. And so that you may understand and know the happiness that you have and that I wish to give you, it is well that you recognize your very nature and it is this: You are mortal and subject to suffering, illnesses, hardships, sadnesses, hunger, thirst, weariness, and much wretchedness. And animals can harm you; serpents can bite and poison you; fire can burn you; water drown you: and finally, you will become old and die and cease to exist. And because of your very nature, since you are formed of both body and soul, there can be within you great struggle and rebellion between the body and the soul. The inclinations of the body and the desires of the soul are contrary to one another. So that from without and from within, you are subject to much great wretchedness, anguish, and tribulation.

"But since I am your Creator and love you as my children and creatures, which you are, I desire to do you great good. And for this special grace or favor I want to concede you one privilege, which is original justice. And from now on I grant you as this special favor, contrary to the quality of your nature, that not one of the things I have mentioned can disturb you or injure you or harm you, nor can anything come against your will that might vex you. And you will retain this special grace as long as you remain firm and persevering in keeping the law that I shall give you. And the law that I give you and order you to keep is as follows:

"You may eat of all the fruits that are in this garden, which are innumerable, as you can see. Only you shall not eat of the tree of knowledge of good and evil, which is planted in the middle of Paradise, for in the same hour in which you eat of it, you will die, and this is because you are mortal, and you will come to die from necessity. Then there will come upon you all those evils to which you are subject according to your nature, which are those things that have been described to you. And so that you may have a stronger will to keep this commandment, I want to tell you more particularly of the happiness which you will have if you keep my commandments, and if you shall not eat of the fruit of that tree of the knowledge of good and of evil.

"The first is that you will be immortal and you will never die, nor will you ever be ill, nor can there ever come to you any pain or fatigue or weariness, or grief or sadness or cold or heat that will cause you pain; nor can any animal or serpent or any other creature harm you. And even more, for all these animals, birds, and fishes will be obedient to you and will do what you command them to do. And you, Eve, shall bring forth your children without pain or suffering. You shall have all the things that you need for your lives and for your pleasure, without any work whatsoever. And even more, you shall have this delightful Paradise as your perpetual inheritance, for yourselves, and for all of those who are born from you throughout the time that you live in this world.

"And all these things I give you and shall give you are not only for you but, also, for all those who descend from you. And even more, for I shall arrange that after you go on multiplying and filling this place, I shall take away a few at a time and carry you to Heaven to my house in body and in soul, without your dying. And I shall give you as your perpetual inheritance those seats and houses that the evil angels lost when they fell from Heaven because of their sin. And I shall do this great favor, not only to you but, also, to all of those who descend from you, until all those places that are now vacant shall be filled. There in Heaven you shall have so much glory and more and finer things than the eye ever saw, or the heart ever dreamed of.

"But if you should break this commandment that I give you, and if you should eat of the fruit of that tree, I shall take from you, and from all of those who descend from you, all the favors and privileges that I have described, and you shall be mortal, and, of necessity, you shall come to die. You shall be stripped of original justice, and you will lose all my favors, and you will be subject to all the misery and suffering of your nature, and of these sufferings you have already heard. And I shall throw you out of this Paradise forever so that never will you or your descendents again enter into it. And when you die, all your souls, and the souls of those who descend from you, will go to Hell, and they shall never leave therefrom until I may be pleased to change the situation, and this will be only after many years. And there will come to you another evil, for many of your descendents will remain there in Hell forever because of their sins, and they will never deserve to be helped through my justice or through my mercy. You see here [God said to Adam and Eve] the great riches that will come to you and all your descendents if you keep this, my commandment. You also see the evil that will come to you if you should break it. Now, my children, look to yourselves very carefully and remain in peace." And so Adam and Eve remained in that Paradise, amusing themselves and eating of the fruits that pleased them most.

Now, my friends, listen carefully to what we want to say to you. You have already heard how the angels who were bad and disobedient to God were thrown from Heaven and were turned into devils. You also have heard how God created the line of men and women in order to fill those places and seats that the evil angels lost.

Now you must know that when those evil angels, who fell from Heaven and who are now devils, saw that God had created men and women in order to people and possess those places and seats that they had lost, they were very much grieved and envious. They desired to deceive our first parents and to make them sin and break the commandment in which God had ordered them not to eat of the fruit of the forbidden tree. For sinning is no other thing than breaking the commandments of God. And for this purpose, all the devils elected from among their number one demon, the most evil, envious, wise, and cunning of them all, so that he might be able to deceive our first parents, Adam and Eve. He took the form of a serpent, and he waited until he saw that our mother Eve was separated some distance from Adam, and he began to speak to her and to attempt to persuade her to eat of the fruit of the forbidden tree. And he said, falsely, that God had deceived them and that, even if they should eat of the fruit, none of the evils that God had mentioned would

73

come upon them. If they should eat of it, moreover, they would become like Gods, and just as God, and they would know good and evil, just as God does.

He told the woman so many such things that she, deceived by his words, believed him and ate of that fruit. Then the woman was not content in having eaten and broken the commandment, and she carried some of the fruit to her husband Adam, and she was very insistent in requesting him to eat of it. In order to please her, Adam did eat of it, just as Eve had done. And as soon as they both had eaten, they were very much ashamed to see themselves naked. For before they sinned, even though they were naked, they were not ashamed, because they were innocent and without sin. Now they covered their shame with leaves from a tree. They had great fear of God since they had broken His commandment, and they hid among the trees. When God saw they had broken His commandment and had eaten of the fruit of the tree that He had forbidden to them, He came to them and asked them why they had eaten of that fruit. Then Adam said, making an excuse for himself, that the woman had begged him to eat. The woman said that the serpent had deceived her. Neither of them recognized his fault, nor did they ask God's forgiveness for the sin they had committed, but each one of them denied his guilt and blamed the other. For that reason they did not deserve God's pardon.

Since they had broken God's commandment and had not recognized their sin, nor had they asked God's pardon, God sentenced them to be thrown from that delightful Paradise, and He deprived them of all favors and privileges He had given them. Then they became mortal and subject to all the suffering and hardships that we now have. And just as Adam and Eve, our first parents, were stripped of all those good things that they had and that God had given them, just so all their children and descendents have been deprived of those great possessions because of that sin. This is the reason that we become sick and die, the reason we have hardships and afflictions and other ills that we suffer. We would not have this if those first parents of ours had not sinned and had not broken the commandments of God.

My brothers, from what you have heard, you will now understand where all the men and women there are in the world had their beginnings. You have also already learned the reason why we all die, become sick, and suffer so many hardships in this life. And you have learned, also, how all things in the world, in the heavens, on earth, in the waters, in the very heavens, in the very earth, and the sea, and the waters, and everything that exists in them, and everything that we see, and all that we do not see, all this was created and made by God. And He is one: Father, Son, and Holy Spirit, three persons and one God. And so you must believe this fifth Article or acknowledgment of Faith, and it is that God is the Creator of all things.

You have already heard how we have said that the evil angels fell from Heaven because they did not wish to obey God. Some of them fell into the bottom of Hell, and others remained here on earth among us. And they all wish us ill, and they envy us because they know that God created us in order to fill the seats of Heaven that they lost. For this reason they desire to do all the ill to us that they can and to make us sin, so that we will not go to Heaven but, instead, go to Hell with them.

Now you should know that among these devils that fell from Heaven, there is one who is prince and king of them all. His name is Lucifer. All the others obey him. And they all have agreed to try to do us harm. And when a baby is born, this prince Lucifer immediately sends another devil who always accompanies that baby and causes him to turn from his will to serve and love God. And he causes him to sin, and he makes him break God's commandments, and he places evil thoughts in his head and persuades him to commit evil deeds.

But since God is very good and loves us very much He sends a good angel from Heaven as soon as a creature is born, to come and take care of that creature, to guard it and advise it to serve and love God, and to keep His commandments. This good angel, who accompanies each one of us, defends us from the evil angel. You should know, therefore, that when you have a good desire to serve God and to keep His commandments, or when you perform some good deed, this urge comes to you through the advice and persuasion of the angel who attends you. When you perform good deeds that he counsels you to do, he is very happy, and with a great deal of pleasure he represents before God all of your good deeds, and he intercedes before God for you. For that reason you should be reverential and have a great deal of love for this angel who protects you, and you should ask him always to take good care of you, and to protect you from the evil angel, or the devil, so that he will not harm you.

And when you have some evil thought or desire, or when you do some wicked deed, you should know that then you are being counseled by the evil angel who is really the devil who goes with you always. And he has a great deal of pleasure if you think ill, or desire ill, or if you commit some evil deed or sin. For when you are evil or when you sin, he will carry you with him to Hell. And so the practice of demons is to try to persuade us to do wrong so that they can carry us to Hell. And the practice of good angels is to try to help us to do good so that they can carry us to Heaven.

These evil angels who are devils are those who have deceived you and have caused you to believe that there were many gods. And they have influenced you to worship them and to build cues[5] and teocallis[6] and temples. And they have even arranged it so that the honor that you should render the true God, you have given to them. For this reason you have sinned most gravely against God, and you should be punished most cruelly with them in Hell. And since they have wished you ill, they have been most happy at your sins, and, consequently, they have ordered you to cut out your tongues, and cut off your arms, and tear your own flesh, and commit upon yourselves many other cruelties. They have ordered you to kill and sacrifice your children and your slaves and other persons so that you will commit greater sins in doing this, and so that you would suffer greater tortures in Hell as a result of it. All of these things that they have ordered you to do, and that you have done, have been against the will and against the commandment of God. And just exactly what these commandments of God are we shall tell you a little later.

You should see and know that all of those objects that you have worshiped and have regarded as gods are only devils who have deceived you. And, therefore, you should put aside and denounce Huizilopochtli and Tezcatlipoca and Quetzalcoatl,[7] and all the others that you have considered to be gods, for they wish you ill, and they have deceived you. You must also put aside all their images and refrain from making sacrifices and performing all other acts that are connected with these idols. And you should burn them all, and you should tear down all of the teocallis and burn them, because these entities are only tools of the devil, and God hates them and all who make them, and God will throw all of them into Hell eternally.

Turn you ears away from these idols, and cast them away from yourselves and turn your hearts to God, who is very good. And He will receive you and pardon all the sins you have committed, if you repent of them, and if you seek His pardon. He will forgive you quite willingly, since He loves you very much, and He desires you to have great happiness. And, consequently, He does not want you to make sacrifices or to kill anyone, or to harm yourselves, or any other people, or to tear your flesh, or to cut out your tongues. He only wants you to love Him sincerely, as He loves you, and build for Him a church in your town, so that you may come there to entrust yourselves to Him and to pray to Him to forgive your sins and to take you to Heaven.

There in the church you will thank Him and praise Him for the kindness that He has done you, and that He is doing for you. It is God who created you and sustains you. He creates everything that you need. He orders the sun and the moon to shed light upon you, and the clouds to drop rain upon you, and the land to give forth its fruit. When there is anything that you may need, you should ask it of the true God, for He alone is the one who can give it to you. And you should not ask such favors of the idols that are devils and the works of the devil, for they cannot give you any good thing, for that is done only by the true God.

The sixth Article or acknowledgment of Faith is to believe that God is the pardoner of sins. In order to understand this, you need to know what it means to sin. To sin is to do or say or think anything against the will and commandment of God. For you sin when you do anything against His commandment or against His will.

Just what these commandments of God are that you are to keep and not break will be told you later. When you commit some sin or break some commandment of God, you must ask forgiveness from God Himself, for the sin you have committed, since only God can forgive sins. And you must repent, quite willingly, for what you have done and be of a firm mind never to offend God again or to break His commandments. And when thus you repent and ask God's forgiveness, God will pardon you since He is good, and since He loves you as His children, provided you are baptized and confess your sins to a priest who says Mass. God has established in His church this Sacrament of penance and confession, and the other Sacraments, so that through them we might receive God's pardon for our sins. And just what these Sacraments are will be explained to you later.

Those of you who are not baptized are obligated to repent for everything you have done against the commandments of God, and to have a firm desire not to offend Him again, and to have the desire to be good Christians and to be baptized. When you are baptized because of this desire, then God will pardon you all the sins you have committed in all your life up to that hour, without your having to confess them. But those sins that you commit after being baptized, you must confess, as has been said. And so the sixth Article of Faith is to believe that through the Sacrament of baptism and through the other Sacraments, God pardons those who are sorry for the sins they have committed, and who promise to avoid them and never commit them again.

The seventh Article of Faith is to believe that God is the reviver of the dead, and that He will give eternal life to the good because they have kept His commandments, and He will give eternal damnation to those who have not kept them.

And so you ought to know that this world will come to an end when the time is fulfilled in which God has determined that it shall come to an end. Then God will send fire from Heaven above down to the earth and all the earth will burn, so will the sea, and rivers and springs and air. And then all people, animals, birds, fishes, plants, and herbs will perish and die. And all other things that there are in this world will be burned and destroyed. And all buildings and mountains and mountain ranges will be leveled. After the entire world is burned, and all men and women are dead and reduced to dust and ashes, God will send from Heaven His angels who will call and shout out saying: "Rise up, ye dead and come to the final judgment." Then God, with that power with which He created all things from nothing, will again create, suddenly, the very bodies that we now have and that each one had in this world. And our souls shall return, those that are in Heaven as well as those that are in Hell, and each one will enter the proper body. And we shall all be revived, and we shall live again, all those who have inhabited the world since God created the world down to that hour.

You should remember that we have already told you that souls never die, and it is only the bodies, and that the souls always are alive. All souls, since they are alive and outside of the bodies, will return to the same bodies, and they will once more live together, the bodies with the souls as we are now. But there will be a great difference between the good and the bad, because the good will live again, immortal and incorruptible, in such fashion that their bodies cannot suffer any pain, or wound, nor can fire burn them, nor swords cut them, nor can they be harmed in any manner.

There will be also the bodies of the good that ought to go to Heaven, after they are revived and are very bright and shining. For each one of our bodies will shine after it has been revived, much more than the sun. And also our bodies will be very agile and light, because they shall be able to move and fly just as much as they desire, without becoming weary. And so, in the blinking of an eye, any one of us with his body can go as far as Heaven and return to the earth, and go wherever he may desire as quickly and as swiftly as he may wish. And also our bodies will be very volatile, because we shall be able to pass with our bodies through the earth and through rocks and through the sea. And we shall be able to enter houses, even though the doors are closed, without any hindrance whatsoever.

But it shall not be thus with the ungodly. For those who are not Christians, and bad Christians, will be revived with very heavy, sickly, ugly bodies that are racked with pain, and they shall suffer great tortures. And those who are good will be light, and those who are evil on earth will be very heavy.

And our Lord Jesus Christ, the Son of God, will come down from Heaven, all powerful and resplendent, with all the angels and archangels, and with the whole court of Heaven, with all the saints, and He will be there in the middle of the air. All the saints and all those who were good will be lifted up with their bodies and revived in the air, and they will remain in the air with Jesus Christ and with His angels. And because the evil ones are very heavy, they will remain on earth with the devils. And there our Lord Jesus Christ will judge the good and the evil. The good will be on His right hand and the wicked on His left hand. And our Lord will say to the good, "You who have been my friends and who have loved me and served me and kept my commandments and have done works of mercy, come blessed of my father, enter and possess the kingdom that I have prepared for you from the beginning of the world." And then our Lord will take all who are good and will place them with His angels and Himself.

Then He will say to the others, "You unbelievers and disobedient ones who have not wanted to believe in me, and have not kept my commandments and have done no works of mercy, go, accursed ones of my father, to the eternal fire that is prepared for you by the devils."

Then the earth will open and will swallow up all those who were not Christians, all the bad Christians, and all the demons, and they will all fall into Hell together in the fire, where both body and soul will burn forever and ever, and the earth shall close above them. Then all the angels will sing, and all the faithful and saints will sing very softly, and they will play many beautiful musical instruments, and they will all ascend with our Redeemer, Jesus Christ, into Heaven. And they will occupy then all the seats and places that had been vacated by the evil angels who had fallen from Heaven, as you have heard before. And there they will remain forever, in body and in soul, with God in glory and in great pleasures, where they shall never have any sorrow, but only happiness. And they shall have everything that they desired without lacking anything.

And so the seventh Article of Faith is to believe that our Lord is the reviver of the dead and that He will give eternal life and reward to the good because they have kept His commandments. And He will give eternal punishment to the evil because they have broken His commandments. So this seventh Article, or acknowledgment, of Faith is to believe that God is the reviver of the dead and rewarder of the good. And you should know that He will repay and reward you for the services that are done Him, by giving glory and rest to His friends and servants, because they have kept His commandments. And He will punish and chastise those who are wicked, because they have not kept His commandments. And so you have seven Articles of Faith that pertain to the divinity of God. They pertain to the divinity of God since through them we know God to be God.

With the first we know and confess that there is one God and not many gods. With the other three we know and confess that God is in three persons: Father, Son, and Holy Spirit. With the other three we know the powers that belong only to God. You should remember that He is the Creator who created all things from nothing. He is the pardoner of our sins. He alone is the one who can forgive our sins. And He is the reviver of the dead and the rewarder and glorifier of the good.

There are seven other Articles, or acknowledgments, of Faith that pertain to the humanity of our Lord and Saviour Jesus Christ. That means that they pertain to Him and that they must be believed.

The first is to believe that the Son of God became man by taking on human flesh in the virginal womb of the most Holy Virgin Mary. So that you may better understand this Article, you must know two things. The first is to know the reason that the Son of God became man. And the other is to know how He came to be man.

With regard to the first, which is to know the reason why God became man, you should know that all the many ills that came to our first parents Adam and Eve, and to all those who are descended from them, came

upon them because they did not keep God's commandments, as you have heard before. And there were three
of these ills.

First, because they sinned, they lost the grace of God
that they had when they were friends of God. After
they sinned they lost the grace of God and all became
His enemies.

Second, they were, before they sinned, servants of
God, and because of the sin that they committed, they
came to be servants of the devil. For he tempted them
and overcame them, and caused them to break God's
commandments. He captured them just as if they had
been conquered, and he made them his slaves, just as
those you would conquer in war would become your
slaves, and both they and their children would be your
slaves, and they are all your slaves. So the devil, who
conquered our first parents with temptation, made them
his slaves, and all who have descended from them have
become his slaves.

The third evil was that after they died, the devils
carried their souls to Hell, and from there they have
never been able to leave, nor can anyone except God set
them free.

When the all-powerful God saw that all men were lost
and had become the slaves of the devil, and that after
their death their souls were confined in Hell, He
decided, through His great goodness and pity, to liberate
all of them.

Thus God consecrated us anew and returned us to His
grace, and made us His friends, for He wanted to free us
from the bondage that we had been in under the

dominion of the devil. He wanted, also, to liberate our souls from Hell by taking out those that were there, redeeming those that wished to be good, in order to liberate their souls from going to Hell.

In order to do this more completely, He wished, through His kindness, to become a man as one of us, and so the first Article, or acknowledgment, of Faith is to believe that the person of the Son of God became man.

And please understand well that the person of the Father, and the person of the Holy Spirit did not become man and take on human flesh, but it was only the person of the Son that took on human flesh and became man.

And in order to understand this you should know that the Son of God always was, and is, the Son of God, but He was not always man. He was man only after He was conceived in the womb of Our Lady Holy Mary. And this happened a long time ago. And when He became man He did not cease to be God. Because since God is immortal, He remained God, as He always was and became man at the same time. So from then the Son of God is God and man at the same time. It is just as if some man among you put on a shirt a little while ago, and he was a man before he put on that shirt, and after he had put it on he remained a man, but he became a man who was dressed, and now he is a dressed man. So God before He became man was only God, but after He took on our humanity and became a man He is God in the form of a man. Just as a man who becomes a friar was a man before he put on the friar's habit, even though he is now called a friar. So Christ is God and man jointly.

And the Holy Virgin Mary conceived Him in her womb not as other women do, but without sexual intercourse with any man, miraculously, by the power of God and without any corruption, and she remained a virgin as she was formerly. And thus bones were engendered within her flesh, without the corruption or opening of the flesh. And just as the cherry engenders the pit without the cherry being open, so was the Son of God conceived and engendered in the womb of His mother Holy Mary without any opening or any corruption.

For a better understanding of this you should know that when God decided to become man and to take on human flesh from the Virgin Mary, He sent a very beautiful angel from Heaven who was named Saint Gabriel, who spoke to her on behalf of God, and told her how the Son of God wanted to become incarnate in her womb and take on human flesh from her and become man. The angel came with this message to Our Lady and found her in her room, praying, and he told her the message that God sent him to tell her. Then Our Lady Holy Mary responded that the will of God should be done in His servant. And then, at that moment, the Son of God was enclosed in her womb and He took the most pure blood of Our Lady Holy Mary and formed a very small body, and in creating this body He infused in it His soul filled with grace. And the Son of God joined in Himself a soul and body in the unity of one person. And God took on and assumed our human form. And the divinity of the Son of God, in soul and body, is the one single person of Jesus Christ. He was a perfect man as far as wisdom is concerned and as far as body is concerned. He grew in age, because even though He was within the womb, He knew everything that is known now. But His body was not large then. It grew little by little as the bodies of other children grow. And so when the proper time had come when women bring forth their young, which is at the end of nine months, He was born of the Holy Virgin Mary in the form of a child. Then He grew strong and became man. And she conceived Him and engendered in Him all that He took from her, which was the body. We have told you already that neither the mother nor the father begets the soul, but that it is created by God. Only the body is begotten by the fathers and the mothers. And so the Son of God as a body was engendered in the womb of the Holy Virgin Mary. And we say that she engendered Him physically. And so the Son of God, who is called Jesus Christ, always is and was God, and God created Him in Our Lady the Holy Virgin Mary. But He took His human body from her, and before this He was not a man and the Son of Our Lady, but only after she conceived Him physically, and he took His body from her.

And the first Article of humanity is to believe that Jesus Christ, the Son of God, was conceived in the womb of Our Lady Holy Mary by the power of God as far as body is concerned, and that God also created the soul. And you should note that when we say that God "made" or "created" or "said," we always mean all the Trinity which is Father, Son, and Holy Spirit.

The second Article, or acknowledgment, of Faith regarding God as man is to believe that the Son of God was born of Our Lady Holy Mary and that she miraculously remained a virgin when she bore Him, and after she bore Him. Just as she conceived Him physically, she also bore Him physically, but she remained always a virgin and without any opening or corruption, either before the birth, during the birth, or after the birth. Just as the star sheds its ray of light without any opening or corruption of the star, so did the Holy Virgin Mary give birth to the Son of God without any corruption whatsoever.

The third Article of Faith or acknowledgment of God as man is to believe that our Lord and Saviour Jesus Christ, the Son of God, was a man and received death and suffering by being crucified on a cross, in order to save and redeem all men and women of the world.

And so that you may understand this better, you should know that after Jesus Christ, the Son of our God, was born of Our Lady the Virgin Mary and became man, He moved through this world thirty-three years, teaching us His commandments, and the road to Heaven by which we are to be saved. On some occasions He taught this by example and works, at other times by words and preaching.

The reason that the Son of God became man was that as a man He could experience the suffering and torture and death that would save us and redeem us and free us from that death at the hands of the devil, as further on you will be told. If men had known surely that He was the Son of God, they would never have dared to put Him to death, and so we would not have been redeemed or freed from the power of the devil through His death. For this reason our Lord Jesus Christ, the Son of God, did not divulge Himself to make Himself known clearly and manifestly to the people that He was the Son of God. On one hand, however, He showed Himself to be God by working great miracles and doing miraculous deeds. He revived the dead, healed the sick, and performed other marvelous deeds. And, on the other hand, He showed Himself to be a weak and needy man. Many times He suffered hunger and thirst and weariness, and showed Himself to be sad and afraid, and that He had as many afflictions and sufferings as any man. Few, therefore, believed He was the Son of God. Others believed that He was an ordinary man, holy and good, and many held this opinion.

And since our Lord preached and taught everyone, He also reprimanded evildoers for their sins. The good people loved Him and listened to Him quite willingly, and the evil people hated Him and wished Him ill and persecuted Him, because He reprimanded them for their wickedness. They were always looking, therefore, for ways and means to do Him harm and to bring about His death, if they could because they believed that He was an ordinary man, not that He was both God and man. And so they decided among themselves to accuse Him as an evildoer before a governor who was sitting as a judge in the city of Jerusalem. For this purpose they sought out many false witnesses who would give false testimony against Him before that judge. And our Lord, even though they accused Him falsely, never tried to excuse or defend Himself; rather, He desired to be put to death so that He might redeem and save us all.

And His accusers accused Him saying that He had said and done certain things, and that because of it He deserved death. And witnesses swore falsely that these things were true, and our Lord remained silent and did not contradict them. And then the judge, Pilate, handed down the sentence of death against our Redeemer, ordering Him first to be whipped most cruelly, then to be crucified on the cross, and then nailed by His feet and hands on that cross and left there until He should die. And so, nailed to the cross, He died. After He was dead, a lance was thrust into His side, and it pierced His heart. For this reason we have great reverence for the cross, and we humble ourselves and kneel before it, and we have it in our churches, and we place it on the roads and in other places, in reverence and in memory of our Lord, the Son of God, who was placed there. There He died, and there He shed His blood for us.

When we worship the cross, we do not worship a piece of wood, because that piece of wood does not feel or understand the reverence we have for Him. But we worship Jesus Christ, the Son of God, who was placed there on the cross, and in whose memory we still keep the cross, and before which we humble ourselves.

He who created all the world from nothing could have freed Himself from death and could have destroyed and killed all those who tried to bring about His death. But He wished only to die, not after a struggle, but through His own will, in order to free us from the power of the devil and from Hell.

It was fitting that the Son of God should suffer death and passion so that through it we might be freed from eternal death, which is Hell. And the reason is that because of the sin that our first father Adam committed against God, he deserved, and all of us who descended from him deserve, the punishment of eternal death, which is Hell. Because even though the soul is immortal, it is said to be dead when it goes to Hell. Because it would be preferable for it to suffer the agony of death many times than to go to Hell.

And man deserved eternal death and everlasting punishment because the man who was our father, Adam, offended God who is Infinite. And for this reason he was forced to have infinite punishment and eternal death, which is Hell, both he and all of us who descend from him.

And since this debt is so great and infinite, and we were obligated to perpetual punishment and death, no one could repay it or satisfy it except that one who has infinite power and strength, and that one only is God. And there is no other. Only God is of infinite virtue and kindness and power. He only could atone for the sin of our father, Adam, and for the debt and death for which we all would have died eternally and remain in Hell forever. For this reason the Son of God desired to die on the cross for us, so that we would not die in Hell. He gave and shed all His blood as a price and in payment for the sin of our father, Adam, and of all our sins. And so through His death we are freed from the power of Satan and from Hell. And this is the reason the Son of God wanted to allow Himself to die.

And since God as God could neither die nor suffer, nor could He suffer pain or hardship, He wanted to take on our humanity and to become a man, in order to suffer and to die. For in human form He might undergo suffering and death in order to save us and to redeem us, which He could not suffer in the form of God.

We have already told you that Jesus Christ is God and man, and in the form of God He is immortal and His soul is immortal, just as ours are, but His body then was mortal, just as ours are now. And, therefore, when we say that Jesus Christ died, we should understand that it was as a man and not as God. As a man it was His body that died but not His soul, because for the man to die is nothing except that His soul leaves the body. For it is the soul that gives life to the body, and when it has departed from the body, the body dies but the soul remains always alive. And even though the soul of the Son of God left His body when He died, still neither the soul nor the body was separated from God. But they were always together, both soul and body, in God, even though the soul and the body were separated from each other. Just as when our hands are joined together when we pray, and then we separate them one from the other, still they are not separated from our bodies, so the soul and the body of Jesus Christ, the Son of God, even though the soul and the body were separated, are not for that reason separated from God. Rather, they remain joined with Him. Thus the third Article of Faith or acknowledgment of God as man is to know and to believe that Jesus Christ, the Son of God, died crucified on the cross in order to redeem us and save us, and that He died only as to His body and not as to His spirit nor as to His being God.

The fourth Article of Faith or acknowledgment of

God as man that we must know and believe is that after Jesus Christ, the Son of God, died on the cross, He descended with His soul into Hell and His body was buried in a tomb. He then removed the souls of the holy fathers who were confined in Hell because of the sin of Adam.

As we have said, because of the sin of Adam, all good and evil people went to Hell. The evil went to the fire of Hell and other punishments that are to be found there eternally. The good were not sent to the fire nor to other suffering, but they were detained in Hell until God should want to free them and remove them from that place. And since Jesus Christ, the Son of God, conquered the devil by His death and paid the debt that we would have paid, thus liberating us from the devil's power by dying. He descended with His soul to Hell to remove the good souls of the faithful who at that time were detained there. And His body remained on the cross, and His mother and His Disciples placed Him in a new tomb in which no one had ever been buried.

The Son of God as God is everywhere, for He descended with His soul into Hell, and yet He remained with His body on the cross and in the tomb. And although the soul and the body were separated from each other, they were not separated from God. And we would say that although a man clasps his hands together and then separates them, and raises one to his head and lowers the other toward his feet, still both hands are a part of him, even though they may be separated from each other.

So the fourth Article of Faith of knowledge of God is

for man to believe and to know that the Son of God, Jesus Christ, descended to Hell and removed Adam and Eve and all the other saints who were there at that time and at the same time his body remained in the sepulchre.

The fifth Article of Faith or acknowledgment of God as man is to believe and to know that the Son of God who died in body, was crucified and arose from the dead on the third day.

In order to understand this Article you should know that when Jesus Christ died, His soul descended to Hell and remained there with the holy fathers until the third day. On the third day after His death, which was Sunday, He wanted to appear at dawn. He left with His soul from Hell, and brought with Him all those holy fathers who had been waiting for His coming. And with His strength and power as God, He once again joined the soul to the body that had remained dead in the sepulchre. Just as the body had remained dead when the soul left it, the body returned to life now that the soul was returned to it again. And then God gave Him an even more excellent life than He had before. For before He died He could die and be wounded, but after He has arisen from the dead, He cannot now die nor can He be wounded nor can He suffer, and even if He should enter into fire, He cannot be burned. But His body is glorious forever and can never suffer any hardship. Just as He was born of His mother, Holy Mary, most marvelously, and she remained a virgin and intact and without any opening, thus He came, most miraculously, from the tomb without opening it.

So the fifth Article of Faith or acknowledgment of God as man is to believe and to know that on the third day He was resurrected and arose from the dead, glorious, immortal, and eternal. Just as He died in body, so was He resurrected in body, because His soul and divinity, which is God, did not die, nor could they die, as we have already told you.

The sixth Article of Faith or acknowledgment of God as man is to believe and to know that forty days after He arose from the dead He ascended into Heaven in the form of man, both in body and in soul, because as God He was everywhere, both above and below, and in all parts, but He was not everywhere as man. And so in body and in soul He was there on earth although not in Heaven. And, therefore, He could ascend as man and not as God.

You should know that after Jesus Christ, the Son of God, arose from the dead, He appeared many times to His Disciples and to His friends. And He ate and drank with them many times so that they could see and believe that He had really arisen from the dead, so that afterward they would preach about it to all people.

After He had proved to them the truth of His resurrection, He carried all His Apostles and friends up to a high mountain and there He commanded them to go throughout all the world and preach all these things we are preaching to you, just as you have heard them. Then He gave them His holy blessing. And with all of those persons looking on, He ascended into Heaven as man, through His own virtue and power, without anyone aiding Him or lifting Him up, because He did not have need of aid from anyone.

But you must know that when the Son of God, Jesus Christ, went up to Heaven from this world, He was not alone. He carried with Him a great company of the souls of the holy fathers whom He had taken from Hell. At the time that our Redeemer was to go up to Heaven, there came down from Heaven to receive Him all the celestial court, all the angels and archangels, and all those Heavenly hosts; these were innumerable. And they brought very sweet instruments, and they played very sweetly with them, and they sang very soft songs. And so they accompanied Jesus Christ, the Son of God and Holy Mary, and they went up through the air. Then Jesus Christ entered into Heaven with all His company, and as a man He sat down on the right hand of His Father, because as God He is always with His Father and there in Heaven is Jesus Christ, the Son of God, made man as we are.

So the sixth Article of Faith or acknowledgment of God as man is to believe that Jesus Christ, the Son of God, forty days after he arose from the dead, ascended into Heaven and is now seated on the right hand of God the Father.

The seventh Article of Faith is to believe that at the end of the world all of the dead shall arise, and they will come to a valley that is called Jehoshaphat, near the city of Jerusalem, where our Lord was crucified in order to be judged. Then Jesus Christ, the Son of God, will descend in the form of man, because we have already told you that in the form of God He is everywhere, and, therefore, it is not necessary for Him to descend. But in the form of man, He is there in Heaven and is not on earth nor in the valley of Jehoshaphat, nor in any other place. He will descend, therefore, in the form of a man to judge the good and the evil, and He will carry the good to the glory of Heaven with Him in body and in soul to be there forever. And as for the evil who did not keep His commandments, He shall cast them into Hell in body and in soul forever, and they will never leave there, as we have told you, in the seventh Article of Faith.

And so the seventh Article of Faith, of those that pertain to our Lord Jesus Christ as a man, is to believe that at the end of the world Jesus Christ, the Son of God, will come, in the form of man, to judge the good and the evil. And He will carry the good with Him to Heaven in body and in soul, and He will give them eternal glory because they kept His commandments. And He shall cast the evil into Hell and give them eternal punishment because they did not keep His commandments.

These seven Articles relate to the humanity of our Lord Jesus Christ, that is to God in the form of man.

In the first we learn that the Son of God became the Son of Holy Mary, and that He took on human form in her womb, and became man, not through the aid of any male, but through the power of God and Mary who remained a virgin.

In the second we learn that she bore Him miraculously, because Mary remained a virgin.

In the third we learn that the Son of God, in the form of man, died in order to free us from the power of the devil and of Hell and to carry us with Him to Heaven.

In the fourth we learn that He descended into Hell

with His soul, and He removed Adam and Eve, our first parents, and all the other saints who were there awaiting His holy arrival.

In the fifth we learn that on the third day He arose from the dead.

In the sixth we learn that in the form of man He ascended into Heaven forty days after He arose from the dead.

In the seventh we learn that He is to come to judge the quick and the dead at the end of the world, and that He will give eternal punishment to the evil and eternal glory to the good.

And so all the Articles of Faith are fourteen: seven pertain to God as God, and the other seven pertain to God as man.

The Ten Commandments

THERE are ten commandments that God orders us to keep and to obey so that we may be His friends, and so that He will love us well, and so that He will give us His holy kingdom.

The first commandment is to honor and to love above all things the one and only true God.

And you must know that to sin means to say or do or think anything contrary to these ten commandments of God. All of you, therefore, who worship your gods such as Huizilopochtli or Tezcatlipoca, or any of the others that you used to consider as God, sin against this commandment. Those of you, too, who sacrifice any human being, or draw blood, or offer up anything to those gods whom you used to worship, commit a great sin against this first commandment, which orders you to love and honor the one single, true God. Those that you used to worship are not gods but devils who deceive you, and you sin greatly because the honor and service that you should pay the one and only living God you render to these devils. Those of you who honor your priests who served in your temples, you too sin, because all the honor that you pay them is through the love of the devil, and you fail to give it to the true God. And all of you who have idols or anything like them, and worship them, sin in this because you go against the first commandment that is to honor and love the one single, true God. And it is quite right that we should honor and love the only real God because He created us and gives us life, and protects us from the devil and gives us all the good that we have. And He protects us, and He has created everything for our use, and He will give us the very best that is in the whole world, which is His glory.

The second commandment is not to swear in the name of God in vain. And you break this commandment whenever you tell any lie, and when you swear by saying, "I swear to God." They also sin against this commandment who take the name of God in vain in frivolous and needless ways.

The third commandment is to remember and keep holy the feast days. All persons sin against this commandment who sow their fields, or pluck the corn, or carry burdens, or weave cloth, or do other acts of labor on Sundays, as well as on feast days that the church orders them to keep. It is quite right for us to occupy ourselves throughout the week in our affairs, but let us occupy ourselves one day in the week in the service of God and cease our work, so that on that day we may occupy ourselves more freely in His service, and in thankfulness for the mercy and good that we have received from Him. We may serve God by listening to Mass and the sermon on those Sundays and feast days and so commit ourselves to Him. We are obligated on those Sundays and feast days to keep those feast days holy.

And the fourth commandment is to honor your father and mother by obeying them. And this commandment is broken by all who speak evil to their parents or do not do what their parents ask them to do, and do not serve them and care for them in their illnesses, and do not aid and succor them in their need. But if parents order their children to do anything evil or to commit any sin, the children should not obey. And so if they should command them to lie or steal or commit some other crime, or order them not to go to hear the sermons, or make some sacrifice, or worship the idols, or command them to do anything which is contrary to God's commandments, this they will not have to do.

The fifth commandment is not to kill anyone, nor desire death for anyone, nor wound anyone, nor desire to wound anyone, nor do any harm to anyone. This commandment is broken by those who kill or dishonor or wound or defame anyone, or desire to do any of these things or to do evil to any person. This commandment is broken by women who take anything to expel the fetus when they are pregnant, or give such a thing to another woman, or advise her to do so.

The sixth commandment is that you shall not fornicate, which means that you shall not lie with any woman except that one to whom you are married. The man who is married can know his own wife and no other woman. The man who is not married cannot have relations with any woman. Any man who lies with a woman who is not his wife breaks this commandment. And this means he must lie with the one he is married to and no other. This refers also to the woman who lies with a man who is not her husband. It further means that anyone who desires to do these things breaks this commandment. Any man who frolics with a woman who is not his wife, or any woman who frolics with a man who is not her husband breaks this commandment. And if this is a sin, it is an even greater sin if you commit crimes against nature, such as one man lying with another man, because these sinners not only will go to Hell but also Justice will burn them there in a very great fire. And for this reason you must be very careful not to commit such a great sin. Because of this sin, God once destroyed the world, and He drowned everything with a great flood. There remained only a wooden ark with eight people, from whom once more the world was populated. God also sent fire from Heaven that burned other cities and destroyed them because of this sin. Justice will destroy you and burn you and kill you if you commit this sin. Each one of you who commits this sin will be carried away to Hell by the devil, and because of it you will be given great torture. And those who commit this crime against nature with women, or one woman with another woman, will suffer the same penalty, and also the one who permits it will suffer the same penalty as the one who commits this sin.

The seventh commandment is that you shall not steal. Those who take by force or secretly anything that belongs to another, or those who take anything against the will of the owner, break this commandment. Also those who do not wish to deliver up property that belongs to another and those who damage the property or house of another break this commandment.

The eighth commandment is that you shall not give false testimony or lie to the damage of your neighbor, nor shall you say anything evil about any other person, or make manifest his evil, or defame him.

The ninth commandment is that you shall not covet the wife of your neighbor. The man who lusts to lie with any married woman breaks this commandment. And he commits an even greater sin if he should lie with her. The woman who wants to lie with any married man, or who lies with him, breaks this commandment. But you are not to interpret this to mean that you can covet or lie with women who are not married because you also sin by lying with any woman, even though she may not be married, and you sin also by desiring to do so. This also applies to a woman. It also is a sin for a man to lie with a woman who is not married, as you have been told above in the sixth commandment, but it is a greater sin when he lies with a woman who is married or covets a woman who is married.

The tenth commandment is that you shall not covet the property of others. All those who desire to get possession of goods that belong to their neighbor go against this commandment.

These ten commandments are incorporated into two. The first is to love God above all else. The second is to love your neighbor as you love yourself.

For if you have children, or should have them, you would want them to obey you and keep your commandments, and so God commands us to keep His commandments since He is our Father and He created us and He rules us. And He orders us to obey and honor our parents, as we would want our own children to honor and obey us.

You would not want anyone to harm you or kill you, and so God orders you also not to kill anyone or do harm to anyone.

You would not want anyone to approach your wife, or lust for her, and so God orders you not to approach the wife of another man or to covet her.

You would not want anyone to take or steal or to covet anything that belongs to you, so God orders you not to take or to covet what belongs to another. God orders that anything you would not want or do for yourself, you should not want for another.

You will see how just and good these commandments of God are, and they are called the law of God.

These commandments are the road to Heaven. And we must keep these commandments in our hearts, because by obeying them we shall reach salvation and go to Heaven to enjoy eternally the gifts of God.

The Sacraments

YOU already know that it is a sin to break any one of the commandments of God. My brothers, sin is, however, such a great evil that for it we deserve torment of Hell forever and ever. And we lose Heaven and the glory of Paradise, and we become enemies of God, and He places us under the power of the devil so that we will be his slaves.

If, by chance, we should sin against God and His commandments, and if He did not help us, we would remain forever the slaves of the devil and in Hell. For this reason our Lord God arranged through His great kindness and mercy, to leave for us a remedy when He left this world. He not only died for us to free us from Hell and from the power of the devil, but He also left us a means so that if, in the future, we should sin we can attain the pardon of God and free ourselves from the devil. And for this reason He ordained the holy Sacraments, so that through them He may pardon our sins and return us to His path, and free us from all punishment that we deserve because of this sin.

For this reason you should know just what Sacrament means. A Sacrament is a sign of the holiness with which God pardons us and makes us saints.

There are seven Sacraments:
The first, Baptism.
The second, Confirmation.
The third, Penance.
The fourth, the Holy Eucharist.
The fifth, Extreme Unction.

The sixth, Holy Orders.

The seventh, Holy Matrimony.

We said that the first Sacrament is Baptism. Through this Sacrament our Lord God pardons all the sins we may have committed up to that hour, however great they may be. He makes us His children, and as soon as we die He gives us the glory of Heaven. He who dies before he has reached the age of reason, or does not wish to receive this Sacrament and be baptized, cannot be saved and free from the devil, or from Hell forever. But if one reaches the age of reason, has the desire to become a Christian and be baptized, desires to receive this Sacrament of Baptism, does all that one can to be baptized and repents for his sins, and makes a firm decision not to sin again, then that is sufficient for his salvation even though he is not baptized. So if anyone of you should die without being baptized, and yet has a desire to be baptized and is sorry for his sins and has made a firm proposition not to sin again, then he is liberated from the devil and from Hell. But if any small child who does not have the desire to be baptized should die without baptism, this child is lost to one of the divisions of Hell which is called Limbo, where he shall remain forever, without ever going to Heaven or seeing God. You must, therefore, be very diligent to see that your children are baptized as soon as possible, so that they will not die without being baptized and their souls lost.

You should understand that you shall be baptized only once and no more, because if you should be baptized more than once, you would commit a very great sin.

And so that you may take advantage of baptism, you must have strong faith, and believe, firmly, all the Articles of Faith as we have already told you, and you shall be sorry for your past life, because you lived without any knowledge of God, and because you sinned and broke His commandments. And you must have a strong will not to sin again or to break His commandments. And, rather, you should have a very strong will to keep those commandments. On the other hand, if you do not repent for the evils and the sins that you have committed, or if you have any idea of committing any sin again, or if you have any hidden idols, or if you know of anyone who has them, and you do not tell about it and disclose it and bring in those idols that you have, baptism will be of no help to you, because even though you are baptized, you shall go to Hell. So you must repent completely for your sins and make a firm resolution not to sin again. And you must learn and believe firmly the Articles of Faith which we have told you and be baptized, and you shall be saved.

The second Sacrament is Confirmation, which is administered so that a Christian will be stronger and firmer in the Faith, and for His greater glory.

The third Sacrament is Penance. This Sacrament is a remedy for those who sin after they have been baptized. And so that our God may pardon you of your sins you shall do as follows: First, you shall repent of your sins and evil deeds that you have thought and spoken and committed. Second, you shall resolve not to commit these sins again. And third, you shall come to the priest, the confessor, and confess all your evil thoughts, evil words, and evil deeds, as you kneel before the confessor and make the sign of the cross.

After you confess, the priest will absolve you of your sins, through the power that God gave him to give absolution and to pardon sins when the bishop ordained him and made him a priest. Our Lord God, through this confession and absolution of the confessor, and with your repentance and firm purpose not to sin again, will pardon you of all your guilt and sins that you have committed.

Then you must know that each one of you, men and women, is obligated to make a confession at least once each year. Also you must make a confession when you have some serious illness or are in danger of death.

The fourth Sacrament is the Eucharist or the Sacrament of the Mass. So that you may understand the real value of the Sacrament, you must know that our Lord Jesus Christ, the Son of God, wished to undergo His passion and die for us. And so, that night before He died He celebrated the Last Supper with His Disciples, and He washed their feet with His hands, and He dried them with a piece of cloth, and afterwards He sat down with them again. He wished to show the great love that He had for us, and He desired to leave a memory of such a great love and the painful passion that He suffered for us. And so He instituted and ordained this Sacrament of the Eucharist or the Mass.

This Sacrament of the Eucharist is our Redeemer

Himself, the Son of God who is God and man indeed.

And it was in this manner that our Lord Jesus Christ, the Son of God, was at that supper seated with His Disciples. And when He saw that the hour of His death and passion was approaching, He took a part of that bread that was on the table, and He said over the bread some words of very great virtue, and so miraculous, that when He spoke those words, suddenly that bread turned into His body, into the body of our Redeemer, Jesus Christ. Then He took the cup or glass in which they had been drinking wine, and He said over that wine other holy words, and because of the power of those words that wine turned into His own precious blood. So that the bread and wine over which He said those great and holy words became, then, the body and blood of our Lord Jesus Christ, and Christ Himself was indeed in the form of bread and wine, just as much as He was both the true God and man at the same time. When He had made the transubstantiation of the bread and wine into His body and blood, the color, taste, or odor of the bread and wine did not change. But now, with those new qualities, the substance of the bread and wine were converted into the body and blood of our Lord Jesus Christ, in such a manner that there was the whole Christ, God and man, body and soul.

As soon as He had done this and had consecrated this holy Sacrament, as has been said, He took His own body in the form of bread, and His blood, in the form of wine, for it was already the Son of God incarnate, although it seemed to be bread and wine. It was no longer bread or wine, but it was His body and blood and soul and divinity, for it was the very Son of God. And so taking the consecrated elements in His holy hands, He divided them among His Disciples and He gave them to eat and to drink. He gave them to eat and to drink what seemed to be bread and wine but was not bread or wine, but was the very Son of God, Jesus Christ, God and man, His body and blood. In that holy Sacrament, in the form of bread and wine, the Disciples received our Redeemer. Even though each one of them ate of Him completely, His body was not broken to pieces, nor was it injured. But they received Him and ate of Him miraculously. In such a manner the Son of God, when they ate of Him entered into their souls entirely, filling them with grace and with virtue. For they were given food and drink, which were the body and blood of our Redeemer, as food for the soul alone and not for the body. And so each one of His Disciples received our Lord that night and they ate of Him but, at the same time, our Lord remained alive with them. For our Lord Jesus Christ was able to perform this great miracle of being there whole, living, and sound, and He could be completely in many places, as He is everywhere in the form of bread and wine that He consecrated.

Our Lord, the Son of God, not only performed such a great miracle, which was to turn that bread and wine into His own body and blood and person with those words that He spoke, but He also gave power to all priests to do the same thing. Any priest, ordained by the bishop, who says Mass and speaks those words that our Lord spoke over the bread and the wine that he has there before him—that is the host and the chalice where the wine is—does the same thing that our Lord did. He converts the bread and wine into the body and blood of the Son of God, Christ, our Redeemer, through the power of those words. And that is what priests and holy fathers do when in their vestments they say Mass at the altar. Then they speak those marvelous words that our Lord spoke over the wine in the chalice, and over the white host, which is bread made of wheat. Then the substance of the bread and wine are converted into the substance of the body and blood of our Redeemer. But the bread and wine do not change color or taste or form, but remain with those new qualities, in taste and in odor and in color of bread and wine. Yet they are no longer bread and wine, but really our Lord Jesus Christ, the Son of God who is truly God and man at the same time.

For this reason, when you hear Mass and see that the priest elevates the host which seems to be white, you must adore it as the Son of God, not directing your adoration toward the whiteness that you see, but to the Son of God, Jesus Christ, you believe to be contained in that whiteness: for indeed that whiteness is not of the body of Christ. But it is there without any character in itself. The host, which was bread, is no longer bread, nor is the whiteness a part of it, nor is it the body of Christ. But you must believe that Jesus Christ, the Son of God, is there and you must adore Him, because the contents beneath that whiteness is really Jesus Christ, the Son of God, God and man indeed. And when the chalice is elevated you must do the same thing and adore the blood that is in it, for it is Jesus Christ. Because in that blood is the Son of God, truly God and truly man.

For this reason at Mass you must conduct yourself

with great reverence and adore the host and the chalice with great devotion, because in it is the Son of God, the true God and man. You must believe this and hold to it firmly, because if you do not believe it, you cannot be saved. And so, during Mass you must conduct yourself with as much reverence as if you were really looking upon the Son of God. And you must remain there until the priest consumes and eats the host and drinks the blood, for it is all our Lord, the Son of God, who is in that place, and it is there that the priest receives him. And all priests who say Mass do this same thing.

Even though there are many who say Mass and who receive our Lord in that form of bread and wine, yet our Lord is not divided or made into many, nor is he reduced in number. But He always remains one, and is entire in all places, and each one of those who receives Him, receives Him completely. And through His great power, Jesus Christ, the Son of God, was able to do this.

And you must know that each Christian, after he has faith in, and knowledge of, that holy Sacrament, believes firmly that the host and blood is the Son of God, Jesus Christ, and is obligated each year at least once to receive that consecrated host, which is Jesus Christ, the Son of God. And when anyone receives that Sacrament, he receives Jesus Christ, the Son of God.

You must also know that after you have become good Christians, you must receive the Eucharist each year at the time of Easter. And when you receive this most holy Sacrament with the proper preparation of your soul and confess your sins and repent for them and intend not to sin again, you receive the great grace of God.

And when you receive that consecrated host, you receive Jesus Christ, the Son of God. After you receive Him, He remains always in your soul, lodged by grace there as if in His own house. And He remains there, always, and never departs unless you sin again. But if you sin and break any of His commandments, then He departs from your soul, and removes from you His grace that He had given you. And then the devil comes and takes up lodging there. For this reason you should be very careful not to sin, because through sin you expel God from your soul and take in the devil. And for this reason this Sacrament is given to us and we receive it, so that through it we may become even closer friends of God, and receive Him in our souls that we may have Him dwelling there forever.

You must know that when, with devotion and with proper preparation, you receive this holy Sacrament, and when you guard against sinning by reverence, our Lord, the Son of God, who is in your soul, pardons you of your sins, and conceives a very deep love for you, and protects you from the devil by night and by day. And when He is in your soul, and in your presence, the holy angels accompany Him, for they are always with their Creator and Master. And since He is there, He gives you good thoughts, and He assists you in performing good deeds. And since He is there the devils flee, for they do not dare to approach you. But when you sin and break some commandment of God, then Jesus Christ, the Son of God, departs from your soul and with Him go the angels who always accompany Him, leaving your soul completely unprotected. And the devils enter into you, and they are the ones who inspire evil thoughts in you, and they encourage you to do evil. For this reason you must be very careful not to sin.

In the Sacrament of the Eucharist, or the Mass, you should notice just how great was the love that our Lord had for us. Not only was He willing to die for us as He did die, but He wanted to leave us in this Sacrament His body and His blood and His very being, so that He might be with us always and we with Him, and that we might receive Him every time that we should have need of Him. And even though He ascended into Heaven, yet He does not fail to be with us here, because our Lord can be in Heaven and also can be here in the Sacrament of the Eucharist and consecrated host. And not only can He be in one place, He can also be in many places. And for this reason, you and we, and all Christians, ought to love and serve Jesus Christ, the Son of God, because He loved us so much and did so much for us.

The fifth Sacrament is Extreme Unction. This Sacrament is administered to those who are dying, and it is sufficient for the pardon of sins.

The sixth Sacrament is Holy Orders. Holy Orders are conferred upon those who are to be ministers of the church, and who shall say Mass, and administer the other Sacraments.

The seventh Sacrament is Holy Matrimony. And this is what Matrimony is: a man must marry only one woman, with the firm purpose not to leave her until death. Both of them must be baptized. They cannot be relatives within the fourth degree. However, there is a dispensation for Indians who are already married in the third degree. The man cannot marry any relative of his, nor can the woman marry a relative of hers within this degree. And if any of these conditions is lacking, the marriage is not valid. Husband and wife must remain faithful to each other in such fashion that he will not know another woman, nor she another man. A man and a woman cannot be married secretly, nor according to the ceremonies that they once used. First, you must find out if there is any impediment such as those already mentioned. Then the church requires that the bans be made public. The priest will marry you, and he will speak to you as follows: "Do you, Juan, give yourself as a husband and spouse to Juana?" And he shall respond, "I do." And "do you, Juana, give yourself as a wife and spouse to Juan?" And she shall respond "I do." And after the question is asked and the answer is given and they are satisfactory, you will be married. And before this time you shall not couple with, or have anything to do with her until you have been married first, in this fashion, and have received the blessing of the church that the holy father will give you at Mass.

The degrees of kinship in which the church forbids marriage are the following:

The first is between brother and sister. The second is between the children of these brothers or sisters who are called first cousins. The third, is between second cousins. The fourth, is between children of the latter who are called third cousins. These cannot marry each other. Nor can those of the first degree marry those of the last degree or anyone in between, according to the common law. But by a special dispensation that the Pope has given to the Indians, those who were married in their infidelity can remain so and might be married as far as the third degree. Those in a lesser degree of kinship can marry. Nor can anyone marry the wives of men of such degree or women they have known, even though the husbands are dead.

Corporal Works of Mercy

PLEASE understand also, my brothers, that you must be very merciful. Mercy is compassion or sorrow that one has for the misfortune of his neighbor, combined with the desire and the will to help him and to assist him, as you yourself would want to be assisted and aided in your need and necessity and wretchedness. So that you may better understand this, you must know and understand that in our bodies we have seven lacks or seven needs, and we have just as many needs in our souls.

The first want and need of our body is that we hunger. The second is thirst. The third is that we are not born with any natural house, nor can we carry it with us, for we are born naked and nude. The fourth [fifth] is that we suffer illnesses and wounds and many other suffering. The sixth is that we can be captured and can be made into slaves. And the seventh is that we cannot bury our own bodies, and so we need someone to bury us, to keep the birds of the air and the beasts of the fields from devouring our bodies, so that we may not be hideous and offensive to those who may see us.

Just as we would want someone to assist us in our

need, and as we would want other people to exercise toward us acts of mercy, so also we ought to be merciful toward other people. Thus there are seven works of mercy in which we may minister to these needs of the body that are called corporal needs.

The first work of mercy is to give food to the one who is hungry.

The second is to give drink to the one who is thirsty.

The third is to receive in your house the pilgrim or the stranger who has need of lodging and shelter, or a place of refuge, as we would want other people to receive us when we may have need of lodging.

The fourth is to clothe the naked, and especially yourselves, because it is a very great shame to display naked flesh, especially the shameful places, both in front and back of one's body. Please understand that it is the will of God that you should go around dressed and with your bodies covered. As soon as the first man and woman whom God created in the earthly Paradise sinned, God gave them clothing with which they could cover themselves, because God did not want men or women to go around naked.

The fifth work of mercy is to visit and serve the sick, since those persons cannot help themselves, and just as you would want them to care for you and console you when you are sick and in the time of great illness, also you should have the greatest care for those who are ill in your house.

The sixth is to ransom and redeem the slave who is captive, and who cannot do what he wants to do nor go where he wants to go, and is separated from his land,

and from his relatives, and from his friends. And, therefore, it is a very great work of charity to remove him from his captivity and to set him free.

The seventh work of mercy is to bury the dead. You shall not fail to bury the dead so that the bodies may not be eaten by dogs or birds and may not come to smell bad. And, especially, you must refrain from eating them, because it is a very great sin to eat the bodies of men. And if you do eat of them, you will, yourselves, be eaten by the devils in Hell. So just as you would not want your bodies to remain unburied, nor would you want your bodies to be eaten, thus, also, you must perform this act of mercy toward the dead by burying their bodies.

Spiritual Works of Mercy

THE seven spiritual needs that we have in our soul are:

The first is that we are born without knowledge of God and without knowledge of anything. For this reason the first work of spiritual mercy is to teach the one who does not know, especially to teach him the ways of God. And for this very reason those of you who know the Articles of Faith, the Ten Commandments, the Lord's Prayer, the Ave Maria, the Creed, and the other wonders of God, are performing a great deed of mercy if you teach these to those people who do not know them, so that by learning about God they may know and love God and be saved and go to Heaven.

The second need in our soul is to have good advice in whatever we do. We make mistakes through the lack of good counsel. So the second work of spiritual mercy is to give good advice to anyone who has need of it. And we should be very careful never to give bad counsel, because it is one of the repugnant sins.

The third failing is that we are inclined to evil rather than to good. As a result, we will commit evil deeds rather than good deeds. And for this reason the third work of mercy is to correct and punish and remove the erring one, or one who is doing bad things, from evil.

The fourth spiritual need is that much sadness comes to us from many afflictions and adversities that come upon us. And for this reason the fourth deed of mercy is to console and counsel the disconsolate.

The fifth spiritual need that we have is regarding peace, for we become offended at each other and act inconsiderately. For this reason the fifth deed of spiritual mercy is to pardon those who offend you and have done you harm in reputation or body or estate, and to remove from our hearts all rancor and anger and hatred and ill will. So you do not fail to speak or do good to your neighbor, because God our Lord commands us to love our enemies and to do good to those who treat us ill.

The sixth quality we lack is long-suffering and patience, for we do not bear with one another. And for this reason the sixth act of mercy is that, for the love of God, we should bear with our neighbor in all offenses and other things that cause us suffering, as we should want them to bear with us.

The seventh, is that we need someone to intercede for us with God, because we are not always in the proper attitude so that we deserve to be heard, or because we are in sin, or because we cannot pray since we are ill, or because we have passed beyond this life into death.

For this reason the seventh act of spiritual mercy is to pray to God for the living and the dead, that our good Lord will bring the living to a holy knowledge of Him, and to a state of grace to those who are outside it, so that they may live and accomplish something in His holy service and may be saved. And you should pray to God for the dead, that He will liberate them from the punishment that they are suffering in Purgatory.

For this reason you must know that in Hell there are four separate divisions.

One part of Hell is for the evil who here on earth did not know God and were not Christians. It is also for bad Christians who did not love God, and did not keep His commandments, and did not repent for their sins. In this area are the devils, and the fire, and all other sufferings that you have heard of before, and those people who are evildoers will suffer there.

Then there is another part that is called Purgatory. To that place go all those who have sinned and who have broken God's commandments, and who have repented and confessed. Those who wanted to confess if they could, even though they were not able to complete here all the satisfaction and repentance that they wanted to do go, also, to Purgatory. The people go to that place in order to complete there the penitence that they were not able to do here on earth. They undergo many sorrows and sufferings, until finally they have paid what they should pay for the sins they have committed. These souls can be assisted by us in alms, in fasting, and in prayers that we may say for them. We should pray for these people so that our Lord should remove them from their suffering and carry them to glory. We should especially pray for our parents, relatives, and friends, and for all the others who were baptized. But we should not pray for those others who are in the very bottom of Hell, because they will never be able to leave that place.

The third area is where all the little boys and little girls go who die without being baptized before they have use of reason, even though they may be children of Christians, or Indians, or any other persons. These children are not tormented by fire, nor do they have any other sorrow that they suffer, except never to be able to see God, which is no small penalty. And they are placed at one side where they shall never see God and never go to glory since they have never been baptized. And so you should make every effort to see that children are baptized as soon as they are born, or as shortly afterward as is possible, because if children die without being baptized they will never go to Heaven nor shall they ever see God.

The fourth division of Hell is a place where the holy fathers were when Christ descended to remove them from that place, and it is not necessary to pray for them since they are already in Heaven.

You must know that our Lord God came to this world, and in it He took a virgin to be His mother, and He wanted to be conceived miraculously, and not as other men are, as you have heard before in the Articles of Faith. And He was born of her, yet she remains a virgin to show us what a great blessing virginity is, and how much our Lord respected it since He wanted to choose a virgin as His mother. And after He was conceived and born, He wanted her ever to remain a virgin. For this reason, those of you, men as well as women, who are virgins and wish to remain virgins and keep your integrity, cannot lie with other persons, nor can you commit any other vile deed or lustful act, nor can you desire to do so, nor speak of it, nor even touch another person. And whoever will keep his virginity will do a great service to God, and will do great good for his own soul. Women and men who wish to get married, however, do not sin in doing so.

Also you must know that the different parts of the body are joined together to make the complete body, and at the head they are joined with the veins and nerves. So it is that many persons banded together under one Lord make a whole, which is called the body. In this manner all Christians form one body, one group of faithful Christians, which is called the mystical body. We are all joined one to another with love and charity, so that we must love and give aid to each other.

Indeed, we are all joined together under one head, that is, our Lord Jesus Christ, and with one Faith, and with his Commandments, and with one Baptism, and with one law, and with the Articles of Faith. And this great group is called the Church. This Church is governed by its head who is Jesus Christ and by the Holy Spirit.

And you must know that this Church is a living

organism and joined together with beams and living stones, for we Christians are those parts. And the place where Christians assemble to hear Mass and sermons and to receive the Sacraments is also called the Church, even though it is made up of beams and dead stones, because there Christians join together. And when you say that you believe in the Holy Church, that means that you believe in the body of all Christians assembled, which is the Church, and that it is governed by the Holy Spirit, by Jesus Christ, who is the head of the Church, which is made up of all Christians.

And when our Lord departed from this world in order to ascend into Heaven, He left in His place as governor of the whole Church, Saint Peter, who served as head of the Church in the place of Jesus Christ. When Saint Peter died, the Christians elected another head, and thus when one head dies, another is elected to take his place. This man who is thus chosen to govern the Church is called Pope, and he resides in a city called Rome. And there is only one Pope in the world. All Christians must obey this Pope. The man who does not accept the Pope as the head and ruler of the Church is a heretic, and this heretic will be burned in the fire of Hell.

The Three Crosses: How They are to be Made and What They Signify

AND you have heard how Jesus Christ, the Son of God, died on the cross and how through his death He conquered Satan and liberated us from His power and from Hell. Since our Lord died on the cross, the cross has remained so powerful, that wherever it is carried, there the devil flees. So the cross has the power to repel the devil and cause him to flee. Our Lord Jesus Christ left us this cross as a weapon to overcome the devil, and He also left us His name for our arm and our protection. For this reason Christians everywhere make the sign of the cross and say "Jesus," which is the name of our Lord, and they establish the cross in the town so the devil will flee. For this reason we make a cross on our forehead to expel the devil from our senses, and another cross on our mouth in order to expel him from our words, and yet another on our breast in order to expel him from our hearts and from our thoughts. For since the devil has no corporal form and we cannot see him, we can only harm or wound him with the arms that God has given us. These arms have invisible power and can wound the devil.

How We Must Make the
Sign of the Cross and What this
Sign of the Cross Means

WE cross ourselves in the following manner: We place our hand on our head and then lower it to the abdomen, then we move it to the left shoulder, and from there we pass to the right shoulder. The head signifies the Father, and for this reason we say there, "in the name of the Father." Then we put our hand down to the abdomen, to signify that Jesus Christ descended and came from the Father to the womb of the Virgin, Our Lady. For this reason we say there, "And of the Son." From there we go to the left shoulder, to signify that from the womb of Our Lady, Christ was born and came to the sufferings of this life and to His passion and death. And from there we bring the hand over to the right shoulder and this means Glory. This sign means that after Christ died, He arose again from the dead and ascended all glorious to Heaven. And we say "Holy Spirit," because this was done by the power of God and the work of the Holy Spirit. For this reason the sign of the cross is made with the right hand, which signifies the power of God, and is made with three fingers and one hand, to show that this power with which all these holy mysteries have been made is included in the Trinity, which is one being and nature and one God.

The Sermon to Follow the Sacrament of Holy Baptism

SO THAT you may see and understand these ceremonies that we have performed before you, you must know and understand why we have the holy Sacrament of Baptism, as well as the other Sacraments that cleanse our souls and pardon our sins.

We have already told you that, because of the sins of Adam, our first father, we lost Heaven and God, and inherited Hell and the devil as master. And also we have told you that Jesus Christ died, and His death was of such power and merit and strength that with it He overcame the devil. And He freed us from the devil and won Heaven for us, and freed us from Hell. And no one ascended into Heaven until Jesus Christ Himself ascended there. Nor did anyone leave Hell until Jesus Christ descended there and removed the holy fathers. And even though the passion and death of Jesus Christ were sufficient to remove everybody in the world from the power of the devil, it is still necessary for us to have that strength in our hearts, just as Our Lord provided water for all the rivers and springs and cisterns. It is necessary for us to put water in our stomachs, and it is necessary for us to bring it from the river and from the springs so that we may quench our thirst. And so that the passion and suffering of God may be of some advantage to us and may drive the devil from our hearts, it is necessary that we place that power in our souls. As water bottles and pitchers are instruments or vessels with which we bring water to quench our thirst and to pour into our stomachs, so the Sacraments are spiritual water bottles, pitchers, or vessels with which one pours and places virtue and the power of the passion of Christ in our souls. And because of the passion and death of Christ, the Sacraments have the power to cleanse our souls from all sins and to expel the devil from us. Baptism, then, has the spiritual power to cleanse our souls, and to cleanse children of stain and original sin, and to cleanse adults from that same original sin and from all the other actual sins that they have committed before they are baptized.

Already we have told you how the cross was the

spiritual weapon employed to throw out the devil from wherever he might be, and how it is employed to defend us. And it is for that reason that we make the sign of the cross on all the senses, on the breast and on the back of the one we baptize, so that it will drive out the devil from all parts wherever he might do any damage, and so that the doors of our hearts will remain open to God and closed to the devil, and so that we will be protected everywhere, in front and behind.

Since the devil, which we have expelled from you, will return with greater fury and diligence to deceive you and to return you to his power, you must be wise and discreet men and walk in continual war against him, so that you may be able to defend yourselves from him and conquer him. It is for this reason that we make the sign of the cross on the top of your head and place salt in your mouth, which signifies discretion and knowledge, so that in the future you may be able to arm yourselves with the cross when you lie down to sleep, and when you get up. You would also make the sign of the cross above everything you eat and drink, and before everything you do.

And so that you may know just what the works of the devil are and flee from them and separate yourself from them, you should know all the ceremonies and sacrifices that you have practiced up to now are the work of the devil. Also, not keeping holy days, or coming to sermons or to Mass are the works of the devil. To kill or wish ill to your neighbor, to lust or to covet women, to take what belongs to another, or covet it, to lie, or to bear false witness are all works of the devil.

The works of God help you to fulfill and obey all the commandments of God, as we have told you.

Then you renounce the devil in all his works when you say "Abrenuntio." And then you take God as your Lord and confess your faith by saying the Creed. Then our Lord God receives you as one of His own, and He makes you His children when the father or priest pours the holy water upon you and so baptizes you. Then we dress you in white clothing and give you a lighted candle. The white shirt signifies the whiteness and cleanness of your soul after you have received Holy Baptism. The candle means that your soul has left darkness and has escaped from the deceits of the devil in which you lived, and that you are now baptized in light and in true knowledge of God.

Now your souls are very beautiful and you must be clean within your own souls by keeping away from sin. Your bodies, too, must be clean and intact as God gave them to you and not painted or scarred, and no part may be cut nor can the body be sacrificed. Also, you must wear clean shawls and shirts, because God is clean and wants His friends to be clean.

A Short History of the World, from the Beginning to the End

YOU should know, my brothers, how the world was created, and from where everything took its beginning. We have already told you something of these things, but in order to impress it upon your memory even more, we want to repeat it briefly.

You must know how it is said that the all-powerful God created everything out of nothing. And you should know that the angels, the heavens, the sea, the earth, the fishes, the birds, the animals, and all other things were created in six days.

On the first day He created light and brightness.

On the second day He created the heavens, angels, and all other spiritual beings.

On the third day He created the earth, the sea, the trees, and the fruits.

On the fourth day He created the sun, the moon, and the stars.

On the fifth day He created the birds, the fishes, the beasts of the sea, and the serpents.

On the sixth day He created the animals of the earth and, after he created all these things, God created man, who was our father Adam, and He made his body from mud. He made a mass of earth and water and fire and air, which are the four elements, and he formed from that earth, thus mixed, a figure of a man, and he turned it into flesh and bone and the body of Adam. He created his soul from nothing, not from earth or from air or from any other element, but from nothing, just as He created Heaven, and all other things that He created from nothing. And He placed the soul in the body of Adam, and He lifted him up a living, perfect, and wise man. Then He placed him in the earthly Paradise and cast a great sleep upon him. And Adam went to sleep, and God removed from him one of his ribs, and from it He created Eve. And God converted that rib into the body of Eve, as He converted earth into the body of Adam. And He made a goddess of Eve so that she would be the wife of Adam. That means that the man shall have and marry only one woman, and, as long as she lives, he cannot marry any other or possess any other. And the woman can marry only one man, and as long as he shall live she cannot marry any other. And neither one of them can marry again until one of them has died. But as soon as one of them dies, the one who remains alive can marry again. And so it is that every time that one of the couple dies, the one that remains alive can remarry.

And God formed Eve from the rib of Adam, and not from the flesh, because the flesh is weak and soft and is outside the body, but the rib is strong and hard, and is within the man and near his heart, in the middle of his body. This means that the husband must have more love for his wife than for any other woman, and the woman more love for her husband than for any other man. This love must be strong and lasting, so that nothing can break it, no vexation nor illness, nor any other thing. No dissatisfaction that one may have with the other shall separate them, but they shall always bear with each other. They shall not despise each other, but shall love each other as good companions and brothers and sisters do, and treat each other with much affection.

For this reason God did not form the woman from the head of Adam, because you should know that she is not to be greater than her husband. Neither did He take her from his foot, because the husband should know that his wife is not inferior to him. But He took her from the middle of his side, so that both should understand that they are equal, and they shall live at peace with each other. And so you have heard that after our Lord had created all these things, He created Adam and Eve, our first parents. He created their souls from nothing, and their bodies from earth and water and air and fire.

And you must know that God created all the angels, the good ones who remained in Heaven, as well as the evil ones who fell from Heaven and became devils. They are the ones who up to now have deceived you. God also created the heaven, sun, moon, and stars and the four elements that are earth, water, fire, and air.

And also you should know that God did not give the angels power to beget other angels, as He gave men the power to engender other men. And the reason is that when God created the angels, He created enough to fill Heaven, and since angels never die and the number does not decrease, it was not necessary for them to beget others. For that reason God did not want angels to beget other angels, nor did He want the number of angels to be greater than the number originally created.

God gave man the power to beget another man, because when God created man, He made only one man and one woman. And God created man and woman so that their descendants would fill the chairs and places in Heaven that the evil angels had lost, as you have been told. For this reason God gave men the power of procreation so that they might increase and multiply until they reached the number necessary to fill the chairs of Heaven that had remained vacant. Also, since men are mortal, it is necessary for others to be born, so that the world will still have people before the time that God has ordained that the world shall come to an end, which will be the day of judgment, as you have been told.

God, then, gave power to engender others of its kind to everything He created that is mortal, and that can come to an end. And so God created the first trees, and the first herbs, and the first fishes, and the first animals. And God gave them the power to beget others of their kind. And they have multiplied throughout the whole world and have sustained themselves up to now, and they will last until the end of the world. So God gave Adam and Eve the power to beget others like themselves, and their children to beget others, and their children still others, until we come up to the present time, and even to the end of the world.

You should know that God gave Adam and Eve and other men the power to engender bodies but not souls. From now on you should remember that the father and the mother do not beget the *whole* son or daughter, only the body, for God creates anew the soul in the body of the child while it is in the womb of the mother. But to fishes and birds, and to all other animals that have sensual life, God gave the power to engender souls and bodies of others of their kind, and so their young take the soul and the bodies from their fathers and mothers.

But the children of Adam and Eve and other men do not take from their parents anything except the body, for their souls come from God. For this reason only the souls of men and women who have reason are immortal and cannot die, because God who created them is immortal. But our bodies are mortal because our parents who engendered them are mortal. All other animals are mortal and they die in body as well as in spirit, just as their parents did. And so it is that when a fish or a bird or an animal dies, it dies both in spirit and in body. But when man dies, he does not die completely, for only his body, which he received from his parents, dies. The spirit never dies, for the immortal God created it in His own image. Then He willed that it should be immortal, and He gave it memory and understanding and will.

You should know that the heavens are round and hollow, and that the angels move them through the commandment of God. And within them God created the world and all things that have substance. And the heavens move around, as we see that the sun in one day and one night rises and makes one complete turn around the earth. We see it in the morning, and it moves over us and over this land and water that we see, and in that fashion it moves over all the other parts of the earth and the sea that we do not see. Thus it circles the whole world. And in this fashion it moves until it rises again in the morning where we saw it rise the first time. The sea and the earth form a round body, something like a *batey* or a sphere, and the top of this ball of the earth is between us and the sun when the sun goes down and goes to the other side of the earth. Then the earth hides the sun from us, and we cannot see it. Then it grows dark when the sun moves to that side, and it becomes night. Now night is nothing except a shadow that the earth casts and places between the sun and us.

And you must know that the sun is not a living thing,

nor the moon, nor the stars, but it is a bright thing that God has placed in the sky. Since the sky moves, the sun also moves, and so do the moon and the stars.

Those of you, then, who worship the sun, or who adore it, or who make sacrifices to it, go against the will of God, because you take from God the honor that you should give Him and give it to something that God Himself created. And when you should adore God, you are adoring the sun and making sacrifices to it. The sun is not God. It has no feeling. It cannot hear. It is only something bright that God has placed in the sky, and it lights the world as a large candle or taper that is fixed in one place.

And after Heaven is the place of fire.

And after fire is air.

After air is water.

And after the water is earth.

And God ordered the water to withdraw into the sea where it is now, and He ordered the dry land to appear in those places where He wanted people to live. And so the water withdrew into the sea, and before God had withdrawn it into the sea, no dry land could be seen. And land is beneath the water, except those high parts that God wished to appear.

LAUS DEO

The Blessing of the Table

Nos et ea que sumpturi sumus: benedicat Deus trinus et unus. Pater: et filius: et Spiritus Sanctus. Amen. Pater Noster.[8]

Thanks after eating

Laus deo: gloria sanctis: pax vivis: requiem defunctis: per infinita saeculorum saecula. Pater noster. Ave Maria.[9]

TO THE honor and glory of our Lord Jesus Christ and of His Blessed Mother, here is brought to an end the present doctrine that the holy fathers of the Order of Saint Dominic, named at the beginning of this document, ordered to be made as a catechism and for the instruction of the Indians, as well as a manner of history, so that more easily they can understand, regarding our Holy Faith. And other mysteries have been declared and added by the Very Reverend Fathers: the Bishop of Mexico and Friar Domingo de Betanzos.[10] This document has been seen and approved by the Very Reverend and the Very Magnificent Licentiate Tello de Sandoval, Inquisitor General and Inspector in these parts. This document has been printed in the great and loyal City of Mexico, in the house of Juan Cromberger,[11] may he rest in Glory, and at the expense of the above-named Bishop. The Bishop requests and implores the holy fathers to be diligent in the instruction and conversion of the Indians. And, above all, to preach and make them understand this short and plain doctrine, since they well know the Indian's capacity for learning and their greater need for this than for other sermons that may be preached to them. This doctrine will serve better for beginners, and the other doctrine in the three parts by Juan Gerçon[12] will serve better for those who are more advanced. This doctrine, because of the great religion, zeal, and learning of the author should be held in very high esteem because of the style and manner that it bears toward the Indians, and it will be of great profit to them, and will suit best their capacity. This is especially true if it should be translated into the languages of the Indians, since many of them know how to read. The Bishop of Mexico charges the three Orders of religious servants of God, who have worked so faithfully and been such good examples, to work diligently in the instruction and conversion of these natives, for here it is very necessary. And he further requests them, through charity, to take very special care with the catechism, since it is well known how important it is for their salvation.

The printing of this book was completed in the year 1544.

Notes

Notes to Introduction

1. Bartolomé de las Casas, *Historia de las Indias,* edición de Agustín Millares Carlo y estudio preliminar de Lewis Hanke, II, 381-382.
2. Bartolomé de las Casas, *Historia de las Indias,* II, 381-385.
3. Bartolomé de las Casas, *Historia de las Indias,* II, 438-450.
4. Bartolomé de las Casas, *Historia de las Indias,* II, 489-500.
5. Bartolomé de las Casas, *Historia de las Indias,* III, 99-100.
6. Bartolomé de las Casas, *Historia de las Indias,* III, 374-375.
7. Colección de documentos inéditos de América, XXXII (Madrid, 1879), 372-379. See also José María Chacón y Calvo, *Cedelario cubano. Los orígenes de la colonización (1493-1512).* Colección de documentos inéditos para la historia de Hispano-América, VI (1929), 427-431.
8. Colección de documentos inéditos de América, XI (Madrid, 1869), 211-215.
9. Colección de documentos inéditos de América, I (Madrid, 1864), 237-241.
10. Colección de documentos inéditos de América, XI (Madrid, 1869), 216-224.

11. Colección de documentos inéditos de América, VII (Madrid, 1867), 397-430.

12. Gonzalo Fernández de Oviedo, *Historia general y natural de las Indias*. Edición y estudio preliminar de Juan Pérez Tudela Bueso, I, 138; II, 194; II, 199-220.

13. San Juan de la Cruz, *Coronica de la Orden de los Frayles Predicadores* (Lisbon, Portugal, 1567), fols. 126-129.

14. Fray Agustín Dávila Padilla, *Historia de la fundación y discurso de la Provincia de Santiago, de Mexico, de la Orden de Predicadores* (Madrid, 1596), pp. 120-121.

15. Fray Antonio de Remesal, *Historia general de las Indias occidentales, y particularmente de la gouernacion de Chiapa, y Guatemala* (Madrid, 1620), pp. 53-57, 77-78, 95-96.

16. Fray Gerónimo de Mendieta, *Historia eclesíastica indiana*, II, 363-366.

17. Antonio de Herrera, *Historia general de los hechos de los castellanos en las islas i Tierra Firme del Mar Oceano* (Madrid, 1601-1615), I, 323-326. A readily available modern edition with a prologue by J. Natalicio González, II, 221-228; also see Lewis Hanke, *Bartolomé de las Casas, Historian. An Essay in Spanish Historiography*, pp. 66-70.

18. Luis Jerónimo Alcocer, *Relacíon sumaria del estado presente de la Isla Española en las Indias Occidentales*, Manuscript, Biblioteca Nacional, Madrid.

19. Emilio Rodríguez Demorizi, *Relaciones históricas de Santo Domingo*, pp. 197-267.

20. Rodríguez Demorizi, *Relaciones*, 112-117.

21. *Boletín del Archivo General de la Nación* (Ciudad Trujillo), Nos. 14-23, 1941-1942.

22. Gil González Dávila, *Teatro eclesiástico de la primitiva iglesia de las Indias Occidentales* (Madrid, 1649-1655), I, 177.

23. Fr. Antonio González de Acuña, *Informe a N.R.P.M. General de el Orden de Predicadores, Fr. Ihoan Baptista de Marinis* (Madrid, 1659), p. 160.

24. Luis de Páramo, *De Origine et Progressu Officii Sanctae*

Inquisitionis (Matriti, M.D. XCIIX), pp. 112-265.

25. *Isagoge histórica apologética de las Indias Occidentales.* Colección de Documentos Antiguos del Ayuntamiento de Guatemala (1935) pp. 162-173, 200.

26. José Mariano Beristain y Souza, *Biblioteca Hispano-Americana Septentrional,* I, 340.

27. Ramón Martínez-Vigil, *La orden de Predicadores,* pp. 104-105.

28. Francis Augustus MacNutt, *Bartholomew de las Casas: His Life, His Apostolate, and His Writings,* pp. 53-58, 68, 162.

29. José Toribio Medina, *La primitiva inquisición americana,* I, 94-97; and *La imprenta en México,* I, 13.

30. Manuel Serrano y Sanz, *Orígenes de la dominación española en América.* Nueva Biblioteca de Autores Españoles, XXX, cclxxi-cccxcviii.

31. Pedro Henríquez Ureña, *La cultura y las letras coloniales en Santo Domingo,* pp. 32-33.

32. M. L. Moreau de Saint-Méry, *Descripción de la parte española de Santo Domingo,* pp. 222, 318.

33. Emiliano Tejera, "Gobernadores de la Isla de Santo Domingo, Siglos XVI-XVII," *Boletín del Archivo General de la Nación,* IV (1941), 359-363.

34. Emilio Rodríguez Demorizi, "Relaciones históricas de Santo Domingo," *Boletín del Archivo General de la Nación,* IV (1941), 429.

35. Pedro de Córdoba, *Doctrina Cristiana,* facsimile edition, pp. xiii-xiv.

36. Joaquín García Icazbalceta, *Bibliografía mexicana del siglo XVI,* pp. 66-69.

37. Ramón Marrero-Aristy, *La República Dominicana,* I, 71-80.

38. Lewis Hanke, *The Spanish Struggle for Justice in the Conquest of America,* pp. 17-22.

39. The three papers appeared in *Historia Mexicana,* XVI (1967), 309-319, 320-340, 341-357.

40. For a detailed discussion of the encomienda system see Silvio A. Zavala, *La encomienda indiana;* Leslie Byrd Simpson,

The Encomienda in New Spain. Forced Labor in the Spanish Colonies, 1492-1550, and *The Encomienda in New Spain: The Beginning of Spanish Mexico.*

41. Lewis Hanke, *Aristotle and the American Indian. A Study of Race Prejudice in the Modern World; The Spanish Struggle for Justice in the Conquest of America*; and "Conquest and the Cross," *American Heritage,* XIV (1963), 3-19, 107-111.

42. For a thorough study of the laws see Lesley Byrd Simpson's English translation and study, *The Laws of Burgos, Royal Ordinances for Good Government and Treatment of the Indians,* and Roland D. Hussey, "The Text of the Laws of Burgos (1512-1513) Concerning the Treatment of the Indians," *Hispanic American Historical Review,* XII (August, 1932), 301-326.

43. Joaquín García Icazbalceta, *Bibliografía mexicana del siglo XVI.* Primera Parte, catálogo razonado de libros impresos en México de 1539 á 1600, pp. 10-11; and *Bibliografía mexicana del siglo XVI.* Nueva edición por Agustín Millares Carlo, pp. 68-69.

44. Among the helpful works on early printing in America are Lawrence S. Thompson, *Printing in Colonial America,* pp. 11-12; Arthur Scott Aiton, *Antonio de Mendoza, First Viceroy of New Spain,* pp. 107-108; Román Zulaica Garate, *Los franciscanos y la imprenta en México en el siglo XVI,* p. 45; and Carlos E. Castañeda, *Beginnings of Printing in America,* reprinted from the *Hispanic American Historical Review,* XX (1940), 671-685.

45. García Icazbalceta owned one copy of the *Doctrina Cristiana,* and refers to another sold by R. Hebner in London in 1834, and still to another copy in the John Carter Brown Library. He apparently was not aware of the existence of any copy in Mexico except his own. *Don Fray Juan de Zumárraga.* II, 34; II, 79. Several other catechisms were available, at least two by the famous French theologian Jean Gerson: *Tripartito, si quiere confesional,* translated

140

into Spanish and printed in Zaragoza in 1529, and *Tripartito,* translated into Spanish direct from the Latin and published in Mexico, at the request of Bishop Zumárraga, in 1544. Bishop Zumárraga also ordered another *doctrina* translated into the Mexican language, published in 1548. The unique copy is in the Biblioteca Nacional, Madrid. A facsimile edition was published in Madrid in *Colección de incunables americanos, siglo XVI.* Robert Ricard in *La Conquista espiritual de México,* pp. 220-222, is in error when he says that the Nahuatl translation was made from Córdoba's *Doctrina Cristiana.* He had not had the opportunity to examine both texts. Other catechisms were published in the New World in the first half of the sixteenth century, but only those that fit into the work of Pedro de Córdoba are mentioned here.

Notes to Christian Doctrine

1. Tello de Sandoval: Spanish prelate, born in Sevilla, member of the Royal Council of the Indies, president 1564-1567, visited New World, bishop of Osma, died 1580 in Plasencia.
2. Juan de Zumárraga: Franciscan, born before 1478 in Durango, Vizcaya, named first Bishop of Mexico by Charles V in 1528. Died in Mexico, 1548.
3. Huizilopochtli: War god of the Aztecs, to whom the great pyramid temple at Tenochtitlan was dedicated.
4. Tezcatlipoca: Aztec god of night, music, and dance.
5. Cue: temple of Quetzalcoatl.
6. Teocalli: A temple of Mexico or Central America, usually built on a truncated mound; the mound itself; the Great Pyramid of Tenochtitlan.
7. Quetzalcoatl: one of the principal gods of the Aztec pantheon. A god of peace, the central figure in many Mexican myths.

8. May God bless us and the food we are about to eat. God, three in one—Father, Son and Holy Spirit. Amen. Pater Noster.

9. Praise be to God, Glory to the Saints. Peace to the living. Rest to the dead. World without end. Pater Noster. Ave María.

10. Domingo Betanzos: Dominican missionary, born in León. In Santo Domingo, 1515; 1526 in Mexico, founded Dominican Province of Mexico; disagreed with ideas of Las Casas; offered but refused the bishopric of Guatemala; died in Valladolid, 1549.

11. Juan Cromberger: Famous German printer in Sevilla who contracted to install a printing establishment in Mexico, managed by Giovanni Paoli (Juan Pablos), but never came to New World.

12. Jean Gerson. Jean Charlier de Gerson: French theologian, born 1363 in Gerson (Rheims), author of many famous theological works; in his last years content to give religious instruction to the children; died in Lyon, 1429.

Bibliography

Aiton, Arthur Scott. *Antonio de Mendoza, First Viceroy of New Spain*. Durham, N.C.: Duke University Press, 1927.

Alcocer, Luis Jerónimo. *Relación sumaria del estado presente de la Isla Española en las Indias Occidentales, hasta el año mill seis cientos y cincuenta*. Manuscript in the Biblioteca Nacional, Madrid. Part printed in Emilio Rodríguez Demorizi, *Relaciones históricas de Santo Domingo*. Ciudad Trujillo, 1942.

Beristain y Souza, José Mariano. *Biblioteca Hispano-Americana Septentrional*. Segunda edición, 3 vols. Amecameca, Mexico, 1883. The first edition was in 3 vols., Mexico, 1816-1821. José Toribio Medina published a fourth volume in 1897 from notes prepared mainly by Beristain.

Casas, Bartolomé de las. *Historia de las Indias,* edición de Agustín Millares Carlo y estudio preliminar de Lewis Hanke. 3 vols. México-Buenos Aires: Fondo de Cultura Económica, 1951.

Castañeda, Carlos E. *Beginnings of Printing in America*. Austin, Texas: St. Edward's University, 1940. Reprinted from the *Hispanic American Historical Review,* XX (November, 1940), 671-685.

Chacón y Calvo, José María. *Cedulario cubano. Los orígenes de la colonización (1493-1512)*. Colección de documentos inéditos para la historia de Hispano América. Tomo VI. Madrid: Compañía Ibero-Americana de Publicaciones, 1929.

Colección de documentos inéditos relativos al descubrimiento, conquista y colonización de las posesiones españolas en América y Occeanía sacados, en su mayor parte del Real Archivo de Indias, bajo la dirección de los Sres. D. Joaquín F. Pacheco y D. Francisco de Cárdenas, miembros de varias reales academias científicas; y D. Luis Torres de Mendoza, abogado de los Tribunales del Reino, con la cooperación de otras personas competentes. 42 vols. Madrid: Manuel B. Quirós, 1864-1884. Volumes I (1864), 217-241; VII (1867), 397-430; XI (1869), 211-224; and XXXII (1879), 372-379 were particularly helpful.

Córdoba, Pedro de. *Doctrina Christiana para instrucion y informacion delos indios: por manera de historia.* Compuesto por el muy reuerendo padre fray Pedro de Córdoua: de buena memoria: primer fundador dela orden delos Predicadores enlas Yslas del mar Oceano: y por otros religiosos doctos dela misma orden. La qual dotrina fue vista y examinada y aprouada por el muy R.S. el licenciado Tello de Sandoval Inquisidor y Visitador en esta nueva España por su Magestad. La qual fue empresa en Mexico por mandado del muy R.S. don fray Juan Çumarraga primer obispo desta ciudad: del consejo de su Magestad. yc y a su costa. Año de M. D. xliiii. Con previlegio desu S.C.C.M.

Córdoba, Pedro de. *Doctrina Cristiana para instrucción y información de los indios, por manera de historia.* Prefacio de Emilio Rodríguez Demorizi. Edición facsímil. Ciudad Trujillo: Universidad de Santo Domingo, 1942. (With modern Spanish transcription.)

Cruz, San Juan de la. *Coronica de la Orden de los Frayles Predicadores.* Lisbon, Portugal, 1567.

Dávila Padilla, Fray Agustín. *Historia de la fundación y discurso de la Provincia de Santiago, de la Orden de Predicadores.* Madrid, 1596.

Esteve Barba, Francisco. *Bibliografía indiana*. Madrid: Editorial Gredos, 1964.

Fabié y Escudero, Antonio María. *Vida y escritos de Fray Bartolomé de las Casas*. 2 vols. Madrid, 1879.

Fernández de Oviedo, Gonzalo. *Historia general y natural de las Indias*. Edición y estudio preliminar de Juan Pérez de Tudela Bueso. Biblioteca de Autores Españoles, 5 vols. (117-121). Madrid: Atlas, 1959.

Galindo y Villa, Jesús. *Don Joaquín García Icazbalceta, biografía y bibliografía*. Tercera edición, muy aumentada. México: Museo Nacional, 1904.

García, José Gabriel. *Compendio de la historia de Santo Domingo*. 2 vols. Santo Domingo, 1894-1896.

García Icazbalceta, Joaquín. *Bibliografía mexicana del siglo XVI*. Primera Parte, catálogo razonado de libros impresos en México de 1539 a 1600. Con biografías de autores y otras ilustraciones. Precedido de una noticia acerca de la introducción de la imprenta en México. México: Imprenta de Francisco Díaz de León, 1886.

García Icazbalceta, Joaquín. *Bibliografía mexicana del siglo XVI*. Catálogo razonado de libros impresos en México de 1539 a 1600, con biografías de autores y otras ilustraciones, precedido de una noticia de la introducción de la imprenta en México, por Joaquín García Icazbalceta. Nueva edición por Agustín Millares Carlo. México: Fondo de Cultura Económica, 1954.

García Icazbalceta, Joaquín. *Biografía de D. Fr. Juan de Zumárraga, primer obispo y arzobispo de México*. Madrid: Aguilar, 1929.

García Icazbalceta, Joaquín, ed. *Cartas de religiosos de Nueva España, 1539-1594*. Nueva colección de documentos inéditos para la historia de México. Vol. I. México: Editorial Salvador Chávez Hayhoe, 1941.

García Icazbalceta, Joaquín. *Don Fray Juan de Zumárraga. Primer Obispo de México*. Ed. Rafael Aguayo Spencer y Antonio Castro Leal. 4 vols. México: Editorial Porrúa, 1947.

García Icazbalceta, Joaquín. *Nueva colección de documentos para la historia de Mexico.* 5 vols. México, 1886-1892.

Gerson, Juan. *Tripartito, si quiere confesional del muy esclarecido doctor joan Gerson: Canceller de Paris: de doctrina a qualquier fiel christiano necesaria:* agora neuvamente corregido. Con una breve y saludable introducion del muy sabio y devoto doctor micer Miguel assensio canonigo quondam y vicario general de la Seo y obispado de Huesca. [Fueron imprimidos por mandado del dicho señor: por el discreto George Coci aleman: en la muy noble y leal ciudad de Çarogoça de Aragon año de nuestra salud 1529.]

Gerson, Juan. *Tripartito del Christianissimo y consolatorio doctor Juan Gerson de doctrina christiana: a qualquier muy provechosa.* Traducido de latin en lengua Castellana para el bien de muchos necesario. Impreso en Mexico: en casa de Juan Cromberger. Para mandado y costa del R.S. obispo de la mesma ciudad Fray Juan Çumarraga. Revisto y examinado por su mandado. Año de m. d. xliiii. [Acabose el *Tripartito* de Juan Gerson: El qual se imprimio en la gran ciudad de Tenuchtitlan Mexico de esta Nueva España en casa de Juan Cromberger que dios aya. Acabose de imprimir año de Mdxliiii.]

Gómez de Orozco, Federico. *Catálogo de la colección de manuscritos relativos a la historia de América, formada por Joaquín García Icazbalceta.* México, 1927.

González de Acuña, Fr. Antonio. *Informe a N.R.P.M. General de el Orden de Predicadores, Fr. Ihoan Baptista de Marinis.* Madrid, 1659.

González Dávila, Gil. *Teatro eclesiástico de la primitiva iglesia de las Indias Occidentales, vidas de sus arzobispos, obispos y cosas memorables de sus sedes.* 2 vols. Madrid, 1649-1655.

Hanke, Lewis. *Aristotle and the American Indian. A Study of Race Prejudice in the Modern World.* London: Hollis and Carter, 1959.

Hanke, Lewis. *Bartolomé de las Casas, Historian. An Essay in Spanish Historiography.* Gainesville: University of Florida Press, 1952.

Hanke, Lewis. "Conquest and the Cross." *American Heritage,*
XIV(1963), 4-19, 107-111.

Hanke, Lewis. *The Spanish Struggle for Justice in the Conquest
of America.* Philadelphia: University of Pennsylvania Press,
1949. Also "A History Reprint." Boston: Little, Brown and
Company, 1965.

Hanke, Lewis, and Giménez Fernández, Manuel. *Bartolomé de las
Casas, 1474-1566. Bibliografía crítica.* Santiago de Chile:
Fondo Histórico y Bibliográfico José Toribio Medina, 1954.

Harrisse, Henry. *Brief Disquisition Concerning the Early History
of Printing in America.* New York, 1886. (Privately printed,
taken from the *Bibliotheca Americana Vetustissima .*)

Harrisse, Henry. *Introducción de la imprenta en América, con una
bibliografía de las obras impresas en aquel hemisferio desde
1540 á 1600,* por el autor de la *Bibliotheca Americana
Vetustissima.* Madrid: Rivadeneyra, 1872.

Henríquez Ureña, Pedro. *La cultura y las letras coloniales en
Santo Domingo.* Biblioteca de Dialectología Hispano-
americana, Anejo II. Buenos Aires: Universidad de Buenos
Aires, 1936.

Herrera, Antonio de. *Historia general de los hechos de los
castellanos en las islas i Tierra Firme del Mar Oceano,* escrita
por Antonio de Herrera, coronista mayor de su Md de las
Indias y su coronista de Castilla. En quatro Decadas desde el
año 1492 hasta el de 1531. 4 vols. Madrid, 1601-1615.

Herrera, Antonio de. *Historia general de los hechos de los
castellanos en las islas, y Tierra-Firme de el Mar Oceano.*
Prólogo de J. Natalicio González. 10 vols. Asunción del
Paraguay: Editorial Guarania, 1944-1947.

Hussey, Roland D. "The Text of the Laws of Burgos (1512-1513)
Concerning Treatment of the Indians." *Hispanic American
Historical Review,* XII (August, 1932), 301-326.

Iguiniz, Juan B. *La imprenta en La Nueva España.* México: Porrúa
Hnos. y Cía., 1938.

*Isagoge histórica apologética de las Indias Occidentales y especial
de la provincia de San Vicente de Chiapa y Guatemala, de la*

147

Orden de Predicadores. Manuscrito encontrado en el convento de Santo Domingo de Guatemala, debido a la pluma de un religioso de dicha orden, cuyo nombre se ignora. Colección de Documentos Antiguos del Ayuntamiento de Guatemala, Prólogo de J. Fernando Juárez Muñoz. Biblioteca "Goathemala." Vol. XIII. Guatemala, Centro América, julio de 1935.

The Laws of Burgos, Royal Ordinances for the Good Government and Treatment of the Indians. Translated, with an introduction and notes by Lesley Byrd Simpson. San Francisco: John Howell, 1960.

León Pinelo, Antonio de. *Tratado de confirmaciones reales de encomiendas.* Madrid, 1630.

León Pinelo, Antonio de. *Tratado de confirmaciones reales de encomiendas.* Introducción de Diego Luis Molinari. Buenos Aires: Casa Jacobs Peuser, 1922.

MacNutt, Francis Augustus. *Bartholomew de las Casas: His Life, His Apostolate, and His Writings.* New York: G. P. Putnam's Sons, 1909.

Marrero-Aristy, Ramón. *La República Dominicana, origen y destino del pueblo cristiano más antiguo de América.* 2 vols. Ciudad Trujillo, 1957-1958.

Martínez, Manuel Guillermo. *Don Joaquín García Icazbalceta: His Place in Mexican Historiography.* The Catholic University of America, Studies in Spanish American History. Vol. IV. Washington, D.C., 1947.

Martínez-Vigil, Ramón. *La orden de Predicadores, sus glorias en Santidad, Apostolado, ciencias, artes y gobierno de los pueblos, seguidas del ensayo de una biblioteca de Dominicos españoles.* Madrid, 1884.

Medina, José Toribio. *Historia de la imprenta en los antiguos dominios españoles de América y Oceanía.* Prólogo de Guillermo Feliu Cruz, Complemento bibliográfico de José Zamudio Z. 2 vols. Santiago de Chile: Fondo Histórico y Bibliográfico de José Toribio Medina, 1958.

Medina, José Toribio. *La imprenta en México (1539-1821).* 8 vols. Santiago, Chile: Impreso en casa del autor, 1907-1912.

Medina, José Toribio. *La primitiva inquisición americana (1493-1569). Estudio histórico.* 2 vols. in one. Santiago de Chile: Imprenta Elzeviriana, 1914.

Mendieta, Fray Gerónimo de. *Historia eclesiástica indiana.* Obra escrita a fines del siglo XVI por Fray Gerónimo de Mendieta, de la Orden de San Francisco. La publica por primera vez Joaquín García Icazbalceta. 2 vols. México: Antigua Librería, Portal de Agustinos No. 3, 1870.

Moreau de Saint-Méry, M. L. *Descripción de la parte española de Santo Domingo.* Traducción del francés por el Lic. C. Armando Rodríguez, por encargo del Generalísimo Rafael L. Trujillo Molina. Ciudad Trujillo: Editora Montalvo. 1944.

Moses, Bernard. *Spanish Colonial Literature in South America.* New York, 1922.

Muro Orejón, Antonio, ed. *Ordenanzas reales sobra los indios (las leyes de 1512-1513).* Facsimile text and transcription of the *Laws of Burgos,* with critical commentary. *Anuario de Estudios Americanos,* XIII (1956), 417-471.

O'Gorman, Edmundo. "La idea antropológica del Padre las Casas." *Historia Mexicana,* XVI (enero-marzo, 1967), 309-319.

Ortega y Medina, Juan A.[ntonio]. "Bartolomé de las Casas y la historiografía soviética." *Historia Mexicana,* XVI(enero-marzo, 1967), 320-340.

Páramo, Luis de. *De Origine et Progressu officii Sanctae Inquisitionis, eiusque dignitate et utilitate, de Romani Pontificis potestate et delegata inquisitorum: Edicto fidei, et ordine iudiciario Sancti Officii, quaestiones decem. Libri Tres.* Autore Ludovico à Paramo, Borexensi Archidiacono et canonico Legionensi, Regnisque Siciliae Inquisitore. Matriti, Ex Typographia Regia. M. D. XCIIX. [Colophon: Matriti, Apud Ioannem Flandrum, M. D. XCVIII.]

Phelan, John L. *The Millenial Kingdom of the Franciscans in the New World. A Study of the Writings of Gerónimo Mendieta (1525-1604).* University of California Publications in History, LII. Berkeley, 1956.

Recopilación de las leyes de los reynos de las Indias, mandadas imprimir y publicar por la Magestad Católica del Rey don Carlos II. Nuestro Señor. Va dividida en cuatro tomos, con el índice general, y al principio de cada Tomo el índice especial de los títulos que contiene. Quarta Impresíon. Hecha de órden del Real y Supremo Consejo de las Indias. 3 vols. Madrid: Por la Viuda de D. Joaquín Ibarra, 1791.

Remesal, Fray Antonio de. *Historia general de las Indias occidentales, y particularmente de la Gouernacion de Chiapa, y Guatemala.* Madrid, 1620.

Remesal, Fray Antonio de. *Historia general de las Indias Occidentales y particularmente de la Gobernación de Guatemala.* Guatemala, 1932.

Remesal, Fray Antonio de. *Historia general de las Indias Occidentales y particularmente de la Gobernación de Guatemala.* Edición y estudio preliminar del P. Carmelo Saenz de Santa María, S.J. 2 vols. Biblioteca de Autores Españoles (175, 189). Madrid: Ediciones Atlas, 1964-1966.

Ricard, Robert. *La conquista espiritual de México. Ensayo sobre el apostolado y los métodos misioneros de las órdenes mendicantes en la Nueva España de 1523-1524 a 1572.* Traducción de Angel María Garibay K. México: Editorial Jus, 1947.

Rodríguez Demorizi, Emilio. "Relaciones históricas de Santo Domingo." *Boletín del Archivo General de la Nación,* IV, (1941), 429.

Rodríguez Demorizi, Emilio. *Relaciones históricas de Santo Domingo.* Ciudad Trujillo: Editora Montalvo, 1942.

Serrano y Sanz, Manuel. *Orígenes de la dominación española en América.* Nueva Biblioteca de Autores Españoles. Vol. XXV, Madrid, 1918.

Silva Tena, Teresa. "El sacrificio humano en la *Apologética historia.*" *Historia Mexicana,* XVI(enero-marzo, 1967), 341-357.

Simpson, Lesley Byrd. *The Encomienda in New Spain. Forced Labor in the Spanish Colonies, 1492-1550.* Vol. XIX,

University of California Publications in History. Berkeley, 1929.

Simpson, Lesley Byrd. *The Encomienda in New Spain: The Beginning of Spanish Mexico*. Berkeley: University of California Press, 1966.

Simpson, Lesley Byrd. *Studies in the Administration of the Indians in New Spain*. I. *The Laws of Burgos, 1512;* II. *The Civil Congregation;* III. *The Repartimiento System of Native Labor in New Spain and Guatemala*. IV. *The Emancipation of the Indian Slaves and the Resettlement of the Freedman (1548-1553)*. Berkeley: University of California Press, 1934-1940.

Tejera, Emiliano. "Gobernadores de la Isla de Santo Domingo, Siglos XVI-XVII." *Boletín del Archivo General de la Nación,* IV(1941), 359-363.

Thompson, Lawrence S. *Printing in Colonial America*. Hamden, Connecticut-London, England: Archon Books, The Shoe String Press, 1962.

Valdivia, Luis de. *Doctrina cristiana y catecismo, con un confesionario, arte y vocabulario breves, en lengua Allentiac,* por el padre Luis de Valdivia de la Compañía de Jesús, reimpreso todo a plana y renglón, con una reseña de la vida y obras del autor por José Toribio Medina. Sevilla, 1894.

Valton, Emilio. *Impresos mexicanos del siglo XVI. (Incunables Americanos). En la Biblioteca Nacional de México, El Museo Nacional, y El Archivo General de la Nación*. México: Imprenta Universitaria, 1935.

Wagner, Henry P. *Imprints, 1544-1600, in the Huntington Library*. An exhibition prepared and described by Henry P. Wagner. San Marino, California: Huntington Library and Art Gallery, 1939.

Winship, George Parker. *Early Mexican Printers*. Cambridge, Massachusetts, 1899. Reprinted from *Proceedings of the Massachusetts Historical Society,* XII (1899), 395-400.

Zavala, Silvio A. *La encomienda indiana*. Madrid: Centro de Estudios Históricos, 1935.

Zulaica Garate, Román. *Los franciscanos y la imprenta en México en el siglo XVI.* Estudio bio-bibliográfico por Ramón Zulaica Garate. México: Editorial Pedro Robredo, 1939.

Zumárraga, Juan de. *Declaracion y exposicion de la Doctrina Christiana en lengua española y mexicana:* echa por los religiosos de la Orden de Santo Domingo, Año de 1548. Fue impresa en esta leal ciudad de Mexico, en casa de Juan Pablos por mandado del reverendissimo señor don Fray Juan Çumarraga primer Obispo de Mexico. Se ordeno que se hiziessen dos doctrinas, una breve y otra larga, y la breve es la que en el año de m. d. xlvj. se imprimio. Mandaba su señoria reverendissima que la otra grande puede ser esta: para declaracion de la otra pequeña. Acabose de imprimir a xvij dias del mes de enero. Año de M. d. xlviij. años.

(A facsimile edition of this catechism was published in 1944, in *Colección de incunables americanos, siglo XVI,* Vol. I.)

Zumárraga, Juan de. *Doctrina breve muy provechosa de las cosas que pertenecen a la fe Catholica y a nuestra cristiandad en estilo llano para comun intelegencia.* Compuesto por el Reverendissimo S. Don Fray Juan Zumarraga primer Obispo de Mexico del consejo de su Majestad. Impresa en la misma ciudad de Mexico por su mandado y a su costa. Año de M. d. xliii. [Colophon: En casa de Juan Cromberger. Acabose de imprimir a xiiij dias del mes de Junio: año de M. d. quarenta y quatro años.]

(A facsimile of this catechism, edited by Thomas Meehan, was published in 1928 in New York by the United States Catholic Historical Society.)